# ENCOUNTERS IN MODERN JEWISH THOUGHT:

## THE WORKS OF EVA JOSPE

Edited by RAPHAEL JOSPE and DOV SCHWARTZ

# ENCOUNTERS IN MODERN JEWISH THOUGHT:
## THE WORKS OF EVA JOSPE

Volume One: MARTIN BUBER

Edited by RAPHAEL JOSPE and DOV SCHWARTZ

Boston / 2013

Series: Classics in Judaica

Library of Congress Cataloging-in-Publication Data:
A catalog record for this title is available from the Library of Congress.



ISBN 978-1-61811-265-1 (cloth)
ISBN 978-1-61811-266-8 (electronic)

Cover design by Ilan Jospe
Photo: Eva Jospe, March 1944

Published by Academic Studies Press in 2013
28 Montfern Avenue
Brighton, MA 02135, USA
press@academicstudiespress.com
www.academicstudiespress.com

# ENCOUNTERS IN MODERN JEWISH THOUGHT:

## THE WORKS OF EVA JOSPE

**Volume One: MARTIN BUBER**



**Volume Two: MOSES MENDELSSOHN**



**Volume Three: HERMANN COHEN**

# CONTENTS

# PREFACE

Eva Jospe was born on 12 January 1913 in Oppeln, Upper Silesia, in what was then Germany and later (after World War II) Opole, Poland.

Her father was the president of the congregation in Oppeln. At the age of 12, she and the cantor's son, Alfred Jospe (then 16) became close friends. They realized that they would eventually marry when, discussing a book, one said to the other that there was no need to buy another copy, "because we already have the book."

Eva was a strikingly pretty girl, who looked "German"—whereas Alfred looked "Jewish." Sometimes, when she was seen with Alfred in the street, she would be criticized by passersby who would say, "Why is a pretty German girl like you associating with a Jew?" The photographer who photographed her class displayed her enlarged picture in his shop window, with the notation "A fine example of our German youth." A phrenologist sent to her school as part of Nazi ideology pronounced her skull "the most Aryan" of all the students.

Eva and Alfred were married in January 1935, after he received his doctorate in philosophy at the University of Breslau, and rabbinic ordination from the Breslau Jewish Theological Seminary. Several of Eva's former classmates showed up in Nazi uniform—something that would not have been possible later, but was at the time testimony to her popularity. They subsequently moved to Berlin, when Leo Baeck appointed to the rabbinate of the Berlin *Gemeinde*, a coalition of three young rabbis: the Modern Orthodox Alexander Altmann, the Liberal (or in American terms, Conservative) Zionist Alfred Jospe, and the Reform non-Zionist Ignaz Maybaum.

After Alfred was arrested on Kristallnacht (9–10 November 1938) and incarcerated at the Sachsenhausen concentration camp, Eva took advantage of her "Aryan" appearance and came to the camp, demanding to see the *Kommandant*. While in his office, she saw a row of prisoners pass by, all in striped uniforms and with shaven heads, and realized that if her husband were among them, she wouldn't have recognized him.

Prior to her marriage, Eva had begun her studies in philosophy, and had taken a course with Martin Buber (although she said that the undersized lecturer, in an age before microphones, could not be seen or heard behind his podium). She was expelled from the university as were all other Jews, and never received her degree. Many years later, she renewed her studies of philosophy at the New School in New York. In 1957 the family moved to Washington, DC, because the Hillel Foundations, which at the time were part of B'nai B'rith, moved to their new headquarters in the American capital. (At the time, Alfred was Hillel's Director of Program and Resources; subsequently he became the International Director of Hillel.) Eva then completed her MA in philosophy at Georgetown University, and in 1963 wrote her thesis—published for the first time in the first volume of this series—on "The Concept of Encounter in the Philosophy of Martin Buber." Thereafter, she began teaching modern Jewish thought at both Georgetown and George Washington Universities, and continued teaching at GWU until the age of 80.

At a time when all Hillel directors were rabbis, and all rabbis were males, Eva Jospe did not join many of the other rabbis' wives (she always objected strenuously to the label "rebbetzin") at annual Hillel Summer Institutes or meetings of the directors. Rather, she, participated with the men on an equal footing in the intellectual and professional discussions.

She was viscerally a pacifist, and hated not only violence but also public demonstrations, even for causes, like civil rights, which she firmly supported. Yet, for decades she acknowledged that her son had been correct when, as a teenager, he had pointed out that it was only because of military force defeating totalitarianism that she could live in a democracy as a pacifist, and that without Tzahal (the Israeli Defense Forces) there would not be a State of Israel.

Eva, who came to the USA as a 26–year-old refugee, developed an extraordinary mastery of the English language. She also had an impressive ability to express and to summarize complex issues clearly and briefly in her adopted language. For example, in her discussion of Martin Buber's personal interpretation of Ḥasidism, reflecting his own ideas, and Gershom Scholem's criticism that Buber's representation of Ḥasidism was academically inaccurate and even historically distorted, she summarized the argument by saying that Scholem was interested in academic *research*, whereas Buber was interested in religious *search*. This facility in English and her grasp of philosophy enabled her to edit and then translate into English, selections of works by Moses Mendelssohn and Hermann Cohen (republished in the second and third volumes of this series), and other works (published elsewhere) of Martin Buber[1] and Franz Rosenzweig.[2]

The selections of Mendelssohn's various writings and of Cohen's *Jüdische Schriften* republished in this series are not otherwise available in English. Her 1963 MA dissertation on "The Concept of Encounter in the Philosophy of Martin Buber" has not been previously published, but presents a clear interpretation of, and valuable insights into, Buber's thought. Her several articles, republished in this collection (most of which were originally published in *Judaism: A Quarterly of Jewish of Jewish Life and Thought*), reflect not only the thought of the philosophers discussed, but also her own beliefs and personality. In her article on Hermann Cohen, she emphasized that in contrast with many other "Yekkes" (German Jews), Cohen valued the proud culture of the *Ostjuden* (Jews of Eastern Europe), and she strongly rejected the tendency of Jews after the Shoah to denigrate the innocent belief of pre-war German Jews that it is possible and desirable to live in two cultures—traditional Jewish culture and modern western culture simultaneously. Her article on Martin Buber, like her MA dissertation, focused on Buber's concept of *Begegnung* (encounter), namely that true living is the life of encounter between "I" (*Ich*) and "You" (*Du*), and that the "I" is only complete in relation to the "You." Her article on Moses Mendelssohn concludes with the insight that even if we do not agree with all of his ideas, without his intellectual accomplishments and the

1 Her translation of Martin Buber's "Early Addresses" (1909–1918) was published in Martin Buber, *On Judaism*, edited by Nahum Glatzer (New York: Schocken Books, 1967). Some of this material, and her translation of selections from Buber's *Nachlese*, were published in *The Way of Response: Martin Buber—Selections from his Writings*, edited by Nahum Glatzer (New York: Schocken, 1966).

2 Franz Rosenzweig, *Ninety-two Poems of Hymns of Yehuda Halevi*, translated by Thomas Kovach, Eva Jospe, and Gilya Gerda Schmidt; edited by Richard Cohen (Albany: State University of New York Press, 2000).

example of his life, we would not be who we are today—proud and loyal Jews and citizens of modern culture.

After Alfred's death in 1994, Eva continued to live in their home in Washington, DC, and in her eighties returned to George Washington University, this time as a student auditing courses in Jewish Studies, with professors her children's generation. She had spunk. In the summer of 2002, some months before her ninetieth birthday, she moved to Israel to be near children, grandchildren, and even great-grandchildren. She lived her last years in Jerusalem.

Eva was blessed with relatively good health. Until the age of 93, she had no need for any regular medication and went on long daily walks, though these gradually decreased in distance. Her first hospitalization for illness was at the age of 97½, several months before her death (on 27 Tevet 5771 / 3 January 2011, several days before her ninety-eighth birthday).

We have included in the first volume of this collection of Eva Jospe's academic writings a sermon that she was invited to deliver in 1988 at her synagogue, the Adas Israel Congregation in Washington, DC, to mark the fiftieth anniversary of Kristallnacht—the night when her husband Alfred was arrested by the Nazis. That night was the beginning of the end of German Jewry. She concluded her sermon by saying about the victims of the Shoah, (including many members of her and Alfred's family):

> By our identification with them, we define our own identity. And through this ever renewed conscious identification with those we lost, we may be able to approximate—just barely approximate—the meaning of the expression *Mechaye Hametim,* the calling our dead back to life. Or to put it less presumptuously: by remembering them, we can assure them at least of that place in our hearts and minds that will make them live—live on in us—as long as we do. We can do no more. But we cannot, and we must not, do less.

This was Eva Jospe's belief, and this was her final testament.

Raphael Jospe רפאל ישפה
Jerusalem
27 Tevet 5772 (the first anniversary of Eva Jospe's death)

# ACKNOWLEDGEMENTS

We gratefully acknowledge permission from B'nai B'rith International to republish the following two books, originally published in the Jewish Heritage Classics series of the Commission on Adult Jewish Education of B'nai B'rith:

*Reason and Hope: Selections from the Jewish Writings of Hermann Cohen*, Translated, edited and with an Introduction by Eva Jospe. (New York: B'nai B'rith Commission on Adult Jewish Education and W.W. Norton, 1971). (Paperback edition with updated bibliography reprinted by Hebrew Union College Press, Cincinnati, 1993).

*Moses Mendelssohn: Selections from His Writings*. Edited and translated by Eva Jospe; Introduction by Alfred Jospe. (New York: B'nai B'rith Commission on Adult Jewish Education and Viking Press, 1975).

The following three articles were originally published in *JUDAISM: A Quarterly Journal of Jewish Life and Thought:*

"Hermann Cohen's Judaism: A Reassessment" *JUDAISM*, vol. 25, No. 4, Fall Issue, 1976, pp. 461–472.

"Encounter: The Thought of Martin Buber" *JUDAISM*, Vol. 27, No. 2, Spring Issue, 1978, pp. 135–147.

"Moses Mendelssohn: Some Reflections on His Thought" *JUDAISM*, VOL. 30, No. 2, Spring Issue, 1981, pp. 169–182

The essay "Teaching Modern Jewish Thought" was originally published in *Go and Study: Essays and Studies in Honor of Alfred Jospe*, edited by Raphael Jospe and Samuel Fishman (Washington, DC: B'nai B'rith Hillel Foundations and Ktav, 1980), pp. 115–124.

The essay "Cohen, Our Master Despite Half a Century" was originally published in *Sh'ma, A Journal of Jewish Responsibility* (2/31, April 21, 1972), in a special issue marking the publication of *Reason and Hope: Selections from the Jewish Writings of Hermann Cohen*, with responses by Michael Wyschogrod and Steven S. Schwarzschild.

The sermon "Kristallnacht Remembered" was delivered at the fiftieth anniversary commemoration of Kristallnacht at Adas Israel Congregation, Washington, DC (4 November 1988).

Special thanks go to Eva's grandson, Ilan Jospe, for his cover designs, expertise in graphics, and invaluable advice.

Finally, the publication of these books would not have been possible without the loving dedication of Darlene Jospe, who prepared the camera-ready sections of these volumes for publication, and whom Eva Jospe insisted on calling "my daughter" (and not "my daughter-in-law").

## Editorial Note

We have corrected whatever obvious errors (stylistic, grammatical or terminological) we found, that regrettably, but inevitably, slip through even the most careful of proofreading. However, we have refrained from taking the liberty of changing linguistic usage, such as "man" and "mankind," to make it more gender-inclusive, or such as "Palestine," to make it accord with contemporary political reality. Texts, like history, should not be rewritten in order to impose the conventions of one generation on earlier generations.

# KRISTALLNACHT REMEMBERED*

I'd like to start out with two brief explanatory remarks. The first one is that the person who should address you tonight is my husband, whom Rabbi Wohlberg had originally asked to do so. But he had weighty personal reasons not to accept that invitation. And so I'm standing here as his understudy—something I have actually, and happily, been throughout the blessed years in which he has been my teacher and mentor.

The second explanation concerns the fact that I won't talk to you in general terms about the events the Kristallnacht foreshadowed. Instead, I'll try to give you a feel for the atmosphere in which we lived in the Germany of the mid-to-late thirties. Please understand that what I'm going to tell you is meant to be no more than a personal account of experiences my husband and I largely shared, as well as my own reactions to, or thoughts about, what happened an—unbelievable—half century ago.

Kristallnacht Remembered, as I've named my talk, is a subject that conjures up events and emotions which still haunt one's dreams, but are rarely permitted to surface into one's waking hours, where they would incapacitate one to deal with one's daily business. Yet I do realize that there are times and places which we, as a group, must set aside for a conscious recollection of what happened, and for a renewal of our resolve not to let what occurred *in* the past become merely another thing *of* the past. And this is such a time and place.

Kristallnacht Remembered—two loaded words, each carrying its own burden, each asking us to take upon us, again and again, what has been called "the risk of thinking" (Raspberry, Washington Post), of grappling for meanings that still elude our grasp of re-living experiences we'd rather forget. I should like to look with you at both words, and see what they may signify for us.

---

* Sermon at Adas Israel Synagogue, Washington, DC, November 4, 1988

The first one, Kristallnacht, is, of course, a cynically chosen euphemism and grotesque misnomer. For *Kristall*, or crystal, which, by analogy to the generic name for a transparent mineral is, as you know, a designation of fine glass that has been expertly cut to refract the light into all colors of the rainbow. But what I saw in the early morning of November 10 covering the sidewalk in front of one of Berlin's best-known synagogues (Prinzregentenstrasse) near our home was not *Kristall*, was not cut glass. It was glass that cut, shards that cut into the very heart first of Germany's and then of Europe's Jewry, draining away its life-blood.

How did I come to stand in front of that synagogue? I had run there to find out whether what friends had reported to us in a frightened, and frightening, phone-call a few minutes before could possibly be true. And it was: Our synagogue appeared to be in shambles. The shock of it was such that I could not recall afterwards whether I had seen any evidence of a fire, any patrolling stormtroopers, or any pedestrians. All that registered in my mind, and has stayed there till today, was a carpet of glinting splinters. So I ran home to tell my husband, who immediately left for the Central Office of the Representative Council of Jews in Germany (*Reichsvertretung*), to inform them in person rather than call their switchboard. But they already knew, and in fact were just then attending a hastily called emergency meeting.

What is by now well-known, but was unknown to us then, is the causal connection between those bits of glass falling from the exploding windows of our burning synagogues, as well as from the shattered plate-glass fronts of most Jewish-owned stores throughout the country, and the fatal shooting, a day or two before, of a German Embassy official in Paris (Ernst vom Rath). The shooting had been done by a distraught Jewish youth (Herschel Greenspan), whose parents had just been deported by Germany to their native Poland. Or rather, they and others like them were left stranded at that country's border, because Poland refused to take back any of its Jews who had previously emigrated. In our utter bewilderment about all that had happened, we obviously *could* not understand what we were, however, soon *made* to understand, and in no uncertain terms: the destruction around us was, by Nazi logic, our—self-evidently fitting—punishment for our fellow-Jew's crime.

One day after the Kristallnacht, tens of thousands of Jewish men were arrested all over Germany, and taken to different concentration camps. One of them was my husband. I shall not go into any details about that—fortunately short—period in our lives. But I do want to recount for you some details about his arrest.

Following the soul-shaking morning I described to you, we had spent an apprehensive afternoon at home, interspersed by phone-calls from equally apprehensive relatives and friends. In the early evening, the doorbell rang. I answered it, and was faced by two men in civilian clothing. They showed me their Gestapo badges, and politely asked to see my father, evidently judging me too young to be a rabbi's wife. When my husband joined us in the hall, they told him, again politely, that they had orders to arrest him but they neither gave us, nor apparently knew of, any reason for that arrest. In an almost fatherly way, they advised him to take along some warm clothing as well as a prayer book or Bible, presumably thinking he might have to perform some pastoral functions at whatever place he would find himself. And as they accompanied him downstairs—avoiding the elevator—they asked him in all seriousness whether he preferred to go with them to the main police station by cab (for which, however, he would have to pay), or by streetcar. He chose the cheaper vehicle.

Let me insert here a little footnote, though it interrupts the sequence of events: Some time after Alfred's return from the KZ, he ran on the street into one of the two Gestapo officials. The man stopped him and said: "I can't tell you how sorry I was to have to arrest you." And then, quickly passing on, he wished him well.

But to come back to November 10; at the police station, all men who had been rounded up were held for some hours, again without any explanation, before being loaded into trucks that took them to the concentration camp of *Sachsenhauzen*, near Berlin. In contrast to later developments, it was at that time still possible to obtain a release, if one could submit to the camp's *Kommandant* a valid certification that some country had granted one an entrance permit or visa, which meant that one would be able to emigrate soon. That release was, however, conditional. It was accompanied by an ultimatum in the form of a deadline set for an often impossibly early departure. If that deadline was not met (and for technical or bureaucratic reasons it frequently could not be), re-arrest would follow; a truly dreadful possibility.

In that dire emergency, Chief Rabbi Hertz of Great Britain, who had been informed of that situation, came to the rescue of a few young rabbis by providing them and their immediate families with permits to enter England. And it was our great good fortune that Alfred was one of them. Now we were able to leave with our infant daughter, grateful beyond description that we could escape, and hurting beyond description with the pain of knowing that most of the goodbyes we had had to say would be final. We went first to London, and after a few months there made our way to the US, welcomed by Alfred's brother and his wife.

What I've told you so far happened, as you know, in the late thirties. And that brings me to a question invariably asked of German Jews who emigrated only around that time: "Why didn't you leave sooner? Didn't you see the writing on the wall?" The answer is—as happens so often—more complicated than the question. It depends as much on objective facts—namely the external circumstances in which those you ask of found themselves at that time—as on their inner disposition, that is, on psychological factors.

To some—to take those factors first—it was simply unthinkable to sever all family ties, to leave parents behind, to let children go. (In parenthesis, though, it should be mentioned here that many parents did have the immense fortitude to send their teens or even pre-teens away, entrusting them to organizations that would take them to the safety of other countries, but not knowing whether they would ever be reunited again. And all too many were not.)

To others, the very idea of emigration was inconceivable. They could not bear the thought of pulling up their roots, roots their families had for generations sunk deep down, and to exchange their familiar surroundings with the alien world beyond. Still others were kept from making any efforts to leave until it was too late by a combination of political innocence and an abiding, if naive, hope. Despite an ever increasing number of anti-Semitic laws, they continued to feel that things would, somehow, take a turn for the better. They had seen the Weimar Republic come and go—go, that is, due to what they perceived to be its foolish shenanigans. Subsequently, and misjudging the true character of Hitler's regime, they hoped naively that it, too, would be overthrown soon.

Another group, men and women who had been educated in the humanist tradition, entertained a different kind of hope; it was based on their conviction that the preachments of National Socialism were merely a temporary aberration, running counter to Germany's true ethos, which they found exemplified in the classical works of its poets and thinkers. Putting their faith in the spirit of a nation they believed to represent the epitome of civilization, they disregarded all historical manifestations of an anti-Semitism indigenous to that same nation; they thought they could outlast their beloved country's sudden descent into irrationality, and wait for its inevitable return to reason.

And then there was a small number of singularly selfless Jews who felt that by staying on, they could do whatever good still could be done for their community in its rapidly progressing dissolution. The brunt of this dissolution, however, was borne by those thousands who had indeed, and often quite early, seen the writing on the wall, and had searched in ever growing desperation for some spot on earth that would offer them a place of refuge. But they found no country that would admit them; and so they were trapped.

It is all of these—those who, for whatever reason, chose to stay too long, and those who, cruelly, simply never had a chance to escape the Nazi net that was soon spread across Europe—it is all of those we remember on this anniversary of the Kristallnacht. But what does it really mean, to remember? The word has widely divergent connotations, ranging from the sentimentally nostalgic to the factual or even trivial, from the heart-warming to the heart-wrenching, with many shades in between. More than that; to remember—whether it be done individually or collectively—can, as all of us have experienced at some time or another, be constructive or destructive, therapeutic or traumatic, a blessing or a curse.

Collectively, we are past masters of remembering. We were schooled in this art from antiquity on by numerous biblical injunctions, some expressed positively, for instance in the commandment to "Remember the Sabbath Day, to keep it holy" (Ex. 20:8), some negatively, for instance, in the exhortation to "Remember Amalek," underscored by the added words "Do not forget" (Ex. 17: 8–16; Deut. 25:17–19). But regardless of what it is we are called upon to remember, our remembrances as such have played so pivotal a role in shaping our religious consciousness that Prof. Solomon Schechter used to say we are "praying our history," meaning that the continual recollection of our people's past has become a constitutive component of our liturgy and rituals.

Yet our history-praying, and our remembering Amalek—Israel's prototypical, and perennially re-appearing, arch-enemy—represent, it seems to me, two entirely different types of remembrance. The one is an ever repeated thanksgiving for past deliverances, and/or a reverent rehearsing of past events. The other is—or so some commentators tell us—an explicit warning against all threats to our survival, and to that of the values we believe in. But this explicit warning carries, I feel, also an implicit message, the message I hear resonating in the two small words: "Never again." I'm sure all of us sympathize almost viscerally with these two words. But I am less sure about their real intent: Are they meant to be a categorical imperative, a battle cry, a prayer—or all of these combined?

Whatever the biblical terms *Zachor*, "remember," and *Lo Tishkach*, "do not forget," may mean in the context in which they appear, they must have another, and quite special, significance for us at this hour of introspection, when our thoughts should be turned exclusively inward, when many of us are saying a very personal *Yizkor*. The Amalek we knew has caused us irretrievable losses. As a community, we have been horribly dismembered. We can neither be made whole again, nor can we be consoled.

In hours such as this one, some of us who remember those of the six million we knew personally, can "see" them again, if only with our inner eye, can see and hear them as they once were. And by this mental recall, by our restoring to them a semblance of their personalities, we can save them for some fleeting moments from the oblivion of the mass grave. But how can we "remember" all those we never knew? Though the number "six million" is seared into our memory, it is such an unimaginable figure that it must remain an abstraction for us. We don't know many specifics about the men, women and children that gruesome "six million" comprises. We cannot recognize any of the concrete features that distinguished one individual from the other.

Unable to form an image of what they looked like in our minds, we can, strictly speaking, not truly remember them.

Yet it is incumbent upon us to do so, for they have no one else to say *Kaddish* for them. How, then, *can* we remember our anonymous dead? In the way Jews have always remembered their dead, known or unknown; By affirming, *Yahrzeit* after *Yahrzeit*, our abiding sense of kinship with them. By telling ourselves, again and again that we are inextricably bound to them, so much so that *by our identification with them, we define our own identity*. And through this ever renewed conscious identification with those we lost, we may be able to approximate—just barely approximate—the meaning of the expression *Mechaye Hametim*, the calling our dead back to life. Or to put it less presumptuously: by remembering them, we can assure them at least of that place in our hearts and minds that will make them live—live on in us—as long as we do. We can do no more. But we cannot, and we must not, do less.

# INTRODUCTION

# EVA JOSPE AND MARTIN BUBER: AN ENCOUNTER

Ephraim Meir

Buber was still alive in 1963, he was Professor Emeritus of the Hebrew University,—when Eva Jospe presented her MA dissertation on "The Concept of Encounter in the Philosophy of Martin Buber" at Georgetown University in Washington, DC Maurice Friedman had published his "Martin Buber. The Life of Dialogue" in 1955, which, according to Buber himself, disclosed the inner unity in his work. As a translator and interpreter of Buber, Friedman had acquired for himself a name.[1] Also the works of Will Herberg, Arthur A. Cohen, Eliezer Berkovits and Malcolm L. Diamond on Buber as well as Hans Kohn's biography on the early Buber were available to Eva Jospe, when she wrote her thesis on "The Concept of Encounter in the Philosophy of Martin Buber."[2] Yet, the Buber interpretation was only at its beginnings

---

1 Maurice S. Friedman, *Martin Buber: The Life of Dialogue*, 1955; reprint, Chicago: University of Chicago Press, 1976. Buber was enthusiastic about Friedman's dissertation and wrote a letter for him to University of Chicago Press. In his eyes, Friedman had correctly concentrated his work on the central problem of evil and its redemption. Buber praised Friedman's comprehensive and systematic representation of his ideas. See Nahum N. Glatzer and Paul Mendes-Flohr (eds.), *The Letters of Martin Buber: A Life of Dialogue*, trans. Richard and Clara Winston and Harry Zohn (New York: Schocken Books, 1991), pp. 556–557. Later works by Friedman include *Martin Buber's Life and Work*, 3 vols. (New York: EP Dutton, 1983) and *Encounter on the Narrow Ridge: A Life of Martin Buber* (New York: Paragon, 1991).

2 Will Herberg, The Writings of Martin Buber (New York: Meridian Books, 1956); idem., Four Existentialist Theologians: a Reader from the Works of Jacques Maritain, Nicolas Berdyaev, Martin Buber, and Paul Tillich (New York: Doubleday, 1958); Arthur A. Cohen, Martin Buber. Studies in Modern European Literature and Thought (New York: Hillary House, 1957); Eliezer Berkovits, A Jewish Critique of the Philosophy of Martin Buber (New York: Yeshiva University, 1962); Malcolm L. Diamond, Martin Buber, Jewish

and most of Buber's work awaited to be translated into English. Eva Jospe referred to Ronald Gregor Smith's translation of Buber's *I and Thou*; Kaufman's translation of 1970 was not yet available.[3] Reading Eva Jospe's master's thesis, one has to take into account that works of eminent Buber scholars were still absent. At the moment of her writing, the studies of Israeli Buber scholars of the caliber of Paul Mendes-Flohr, Rivka Horwitz and Avraham Shapira, for instance, had not yet been written.[4] Nevertheless, Jospe's analysis of Buber's thought in this early stage of her academic road, is profound and impressive and, therefore, still readable and thought provoking. As her son Raphael reports, Eva Jospe had attended Buber's lectures in Germany (prior to the expulsion of the Jews from German universities), and thought that the message of his "I and Thou" was an important one: true life is encounter. In 1963, many people were fascinated by Heidegger's existential description of existence as loneliness and being-towards death. Eva Jospe was not carried away by such a gloomy standpoint, she preferred Buber's view on existence as co-existence and as being-towards-life, and characterized Buber's philosophy as "Lebensphilosophie."

In the *Zeitgeist* of the sixties, Jospe appreciated Buber's dialogical philosophy as a welcome protest against an over-organized, over-mechanized and impersonal society. People are more than punch-card holders or workers on the production line; they are more than a cog in the production process. One feels in her work the fear for "the

---

Existentialist (New York: Oxford University Press, 1960); Hans Kohn, Martin Buber, Sein Werk und seine Zeit (Cologne: Joseph Melzer, 1961).

3 M. Buber, *I and Thou,* trans. Ronald Gregor Smith (New York: Charles Scribner's Sons, 1958); idem., *I and Thou,* trans. Walter Kaufmann (New York: Charles Scribner's Sons, 1970).

4 Paul Mendes-Flohr, *A Land of Two Peoples: Martin Buber on Jews and Arabs* (New York: Oxford University Press, 1983); idem, *From Mysticism to Dialogue. Martin Buber's Transformation of German Social Thought* (Detroit: Wayne State University Press, 1989); *Martin Buber—A Contemporary Perspective*: *Proceedings of an International Conference Held at the Israel Academy of Sciences and Humanities,* ed. Mendes-Flohr (Jerusalem: The Israel Academy of Sciences and Humanities, 2002); Rivka Horwitz, *Buber's Way to 'I and Thou'*: *The Development of Martin Buber's Thought and His 'Religion as Presence' Lectures* (Philadelphia-New York-Jerusalem: Jewish Publication Society, 1988); Avraham Shapira, *Between Spirit and Reality. Dual Structures in the Thought of MM Buber* [in Hebrew] ( Jerusalem: Mosad Bialik, 1994).

machine," characteristic of the sixties. Buber's dialogical philosophy was for Jospe relevant and corrective of the American society of those days. In our twenty-first society, technology is perhaps less seen as a threat and a dehumanizing element than as enhancing life and as presenting a new possibility for communication. But more than ever, we are aware of the possible misuse of technology in warfare and of the dangers that linger in nuclear reactors. The dominance of the it-world, the "busyness" and depersonalization is no less prevalent in our century and, in that perspective, Jospe's analysis of Buber's philosophical anthropology, concerned with concrete life situations, remains actual and relevant.

In research, one frequently looks for influences upon one's philosophy. Rivka Horwitz, for instance, emphasized Ferdinand Ebner's influence upon Buber's "I and Thou." Yet, Jospe remarks that, for Buber, understanding of man is more crucial than being original. The teleological aim of the affirmation of the dialogical idea is more important than the archeology of that idea. Buber himself noted that he was not entirely original and that, for instance, Feuerbach preceded him in his dialogical thought. Rosenzweig in his "New Thinking" (*Neues Denken*) also mentions Feuerbach as well as a number of other people of his own time, who developed dialogical thinking.[5] Jospe goes against the trend of pointing to philosophical precedents and notes the originality of the "I-It" concept and the way it was developed by Buber.

Eva Jospe was critical of Buber's philosophy, which in her eyes was not sufficiently rigorous. Profusion, she writes, occasionally came close to confusion. Buber's work is repetitious and, at times, the ecstatic effusiveness obscures the clarity of his thought. Buber wanted the reader to be carried away by his work and to enter the Thou-world. For Jospe, this approach is more characteristic of a work of art than of a work of the mind. Buber's work, she maintains, is rich biographically, but lacks logical strength. Jospe was alert to Buber's philosophical

5 F. Rosenzweig, "New Thinking: A Few Supplementary Remarks to the *Star*," in *Franz Rosenzweig's "The New Thinking,"* ed. and trans. Alan Udoff and Barbara E. Galli (Syracuse, New York: Syracuse University Press), pp. 87–88. Among dialogical thinkers, Rosenzweig mentions Feuerbach along with Hermann Cohen, Eugen Rosenstock, Hans and Rudolf Ehrenberg, Viktor von Weizsaecker, Ferdinand Ebner and of course Martin Buber.

weaknesses. For instance, she asks if a personally experienced truth can become universal truth and if the truth of encounter is transmittable to those who do not participate in it. On the other hand, Jospe remarked that Buber's subjectivity is countered by his belief in an absolute God, the "eternal Thou," who is always present and independent of man. She further defended Buber in maintaining that his subjectivity is not motivated by arbitrariness: he emphasizes the personal freedom and the spiritual. Buber rightly saw that objectivity and intellectual concepts often lack spiritual vitality. Buber, in her eyes, is not a subjectivist, since he does not universalize his own experience: meanings are, for him, always for a concrete person.

Jospe further defended Buber against those who accuse him of mysticism, although she herself wonders whether his phenomenology of the "I-Thou" relationship stands the test of intellectual analysis. And again, in view of Buber's appreciation of everyday marvels, which comes close to Heschel's attention to the wonders in our daily life,[6] she rejected criticism on purely rational grounds as illegitimate. In short: she appreciated Buber's work as spelling out the vision of a charismatic man, with frequent prophetic overtones, a poetic style and a creative language.

Throughout her work, Jospe read Buber *ad meliorem partem,* but at the same time she was critical of his thought. Buber recognized that truth is perceived by people in different ways, but Eva Jospe asks if one has to believe that there are different truths. Moreover, she questioned the Buberian respect for the alterity or otherness of the Other, and his conviction that encounter implies confirmation of the Other's otherness as well as the prohibition of changing this otherness in sameness. I find Jospe's discussion with Buber's standpoint on the otherness of the Other extremely fruitful. She critically asked whether Eichmann, who was a "good family man," or a concentration camp guard, who loved some caged birds, are not rightly hated for their deeds. In her imaginary discussion with Buber, Buber responds that the one who sees a whole being does not hate anymore, and that the necessity of rejection does not equal hatred, but only the recognition that one cannot have an "I-

6 Abraham Joshua Heschel, *Man is Not Alone: A Philosophy of Religion* (New York: Farrar, Straus and Giroux, 1951), pp.1–79.

Thou" relation with all people. To this Jospe responds that otherness may refer to a differentiated being, but it could also refer to someone whose behavior must be rejected as utterly unacceptable. Buber himself admitted in 1953 that people as Hitler were so intensively immersed in the sphere of monstrous inhumanity that an unbridgeable rift separates them from other human beings: acceptance of otherness and any possibility of dialogue with them are impossible. Jospe adds that, in education, if an I influences the Other, there is an alteration of the Other's otherness. In her formulation of the problem of the Other's otherness, she sounds almost Levinasian; Levinas indeed, even more than Buber, based the relationship on differences and on respect for alterity. However, also in Levinas's view, the rights of the Other are limited in concrete society, where all must at least have equal rights. Levinas maintained a high ethical standard, but in his late thought, he emphasized the fact that, concretely, ethics demands a society with institutions, courts, an army and police force.[7] Eva Jospe would probably have agreed with such a realistic approach.

On the practical level, Eva Jospe defines education as interference in the life of another person and as the change from an untutored "otherness" to a "sameness" of behavior and outlook. Against Buber, who wanted "to see the other side" and all facets of the antagonist in order to reveal the potential "thou" in him, she wants people to become different, to return from their wrongness in order to become a "thou." She contests the view that one has to accept the Other's otherness in all cases. She concludes, therefore, that Buber's thought is valid only if one agrees to disagree. Differences may be too great to be bridged by dialogue. She remarks that Buber himself courageously overcame the difficulty of unbridgeable otherness by defying what his people

---

7 For Buber, strategic rationality belongs to the sphere of the I-it, whereas symmetric communication was considered to be the only authentic relationship. He developed a highly anti-institutional standpoint. Levinas, on the contrary, gave great weight to strategic rationality as required and controlled by ethics. He deemed that strategic rationality is needed to minimize evil in the world: institutions were necessary in order to combat man's problematic natural state. See E. Meir, *Levinas's Jewish Thought Between Jerusalem and Athens* (Jerusalem: Magnes, 2008), pp. 112–113.

generally thought at that time: he wanted to have peace with the Arabs and to resume the dialogue with the new German generation.

The short intellectual biography of Buber at the beginning of Jospe's thesis is still worth reading, certainly in what she writes on the influence of Ḥasidism and the Bible upon Buber's thought. However, I would not qualify Buber "a cultural Zionist," but rather a humanistic-religious Zionist, since he wanted the old prophetic ideals be realized in a community of faith that would bring about a renewal of Jewish life in Israel.

Jospe's description of encounter is faithful to Buber's intentions and offers a sensitive reading of his dialogical thought. At the same time, she is frequently critical vis-à-vis Buber's assertions. So, for instance, she asks if Buber's postscript to "I and Thou," forty years later, is satisfactory when he writes about the mutuality between the I and nature. Her position is that he merely rephrases rather than clarifies his earlier statement. The problem of this mutuality remains: what Buber experienced subjectively as a dialogue was objectively the echo of a monologue. Also when Buber speaks about a work of art as "without speech," Jospe thinks that a work of art may "speak" to the one who responds with his whole soul.

Jospe's work is therefore far from a mere repetition or paraphrasing what Buber says. It is a positive, but concomitantly critical approach of Buber. Let me give a few other examples. Jospe points to a contradiction in Buber between the freedom of choice and man's placement in the existential situation of the "*ur*-reciprocity." Discussing the problem of God hiding His face, which is in fact the problem of evil, she notes that Buber's hope of God's reappearance has therapeutic value, but fails to explain why six million Jews were murdered, and why the eternal Thou decided to hide His face just when He was most needed. Those who were exterminated did not see the sun again after its eclipse. Jospe sees a further problem in Buber's treatment of the reciprocity between God and man, if these two entities are forever different from each other, and if God is the absolutely Other. On the pedagogical level, she writes that, for Buber, education is the molding of one's character through meeting a you. If this is true, she asks, how Buber can avoid inculcating values in general, to which he is opposed? And how can we always respond to the need of the hour "*quantum satis*," if the unformed young student needs to know in the long run what is morally right and wrong? Jospe has a series of hard questions for Buber, but she does not forget his great contribution to culture in appreciating his view on encounter.

Jospe explains, illustrates, enlarges and actualizes Buber's dialogical thought. She appreciates Buber's distinction between an ordered world and the order of the world, as well as his writing on the "narrow ridge of insecurity" of the Thou-world, where ready-made answers are absent and where one "sees open country on all sides, with no guideposts to spell out directions." With Buber, she talks about the "whole man" (*ein ganzer Mensch*) in contrast with what she calls the "displaced person." She elucidates fundamental Buberian primal notions as "I-Thou" or "I-it," distance and relation, the inter-human (*das Zwischenmenschliche*), the act of making present (*Vergegenwaertigung*), encounter, communion, speech, listening and turning.

In a separate chapter, she discusses the implications of encounter for various fields: marriage, religion, education and society. Her analysis of these different phenomena reflects Buber's spirit. Marriage is defined as the encounter par excellence, the exemplary bond of a unified duality. The possibilities and problems of religion in their relationship with the eternal Thou are discussed. Buber's view on society is criticized as not realistic enough: politicians are bound by the aim of the hour and negotiating diplomats remain important. Social problems are too complex to be solved by mere talk, and such an approach may even be totally inadequate. In the whole, however, she remains sympathetic towards Buber's dialogical thought. One is reminded of what her son writes in the introduction of this volume regarding his mother's existential attitude: she was a pacifist, but (reluctantly?) recognized that it was also the utilization of hard power that allowed her to talk about the centrality of the soft power of dialogue.

In a creative, but very short chapter, Jospe discusses dialogical elements in other philosophies, pointing to similarities and differences. Socrates' search for the "why" of the world rather than for its "how" corresponds to Buber's criticism of "it" and his emphasis of "thou." However, for Socrates, there are two ways of knowing: not only in dialogical relation, but also in solitude. Socrates' dialogue is in the final analysis also intellectual, and not a state of mind and heart as in Buber. In Hegel's philosophy, the ego and the Other depend upon each other, but the self negates the Other, as in the case of master-slave relation and in intellectual conflict. Jospe notes that this is far removed from facing the Other as a dialogic partner. Hegel's view on the State as the realization of Divine spirit is further contrasted with that of Buber, who claims that the State derives its meaning from encounter. Buber wanted to save human freedom from Hegel's gradual process in history and he set the "you" of the personal encounter against the" it" of the dogma of progress. Jospe also brings into her discussion Feuerbach, who was recognized by Buber as his philosophical precursor because of his view of the social structure of the I. For Buber and Feuerbach, the object exists independently of the subject. Jospe further remarks that Henri Bergson was not a dialogical thinker, but his thought shows some basic parallels with that of Buber. They both disbelieve in the omnipotence of reason, and Buber's encounter as well as Bergson's intuition, through which one participates in the creative evolution, are finally "ineffable." Jospe goes on to compare the thought of Romano Guardini with that of Buber, and concludes that they are close in a number of respects.

Her discussion of the parallels and differences between Heidegger and Buber is somewhat problematic. True, Heidegger perceives existence as existence with others, as *Mitsein*. But I would not conclude as she does that, therefore, for Heidegger, solitude is a deficient mode of existence. Jospe is right in writing that, for Buber, Heidegger's is a closed system, that he is not really a relational philosopher, and that in his system, the Other is merely the object of man's solicitude (*Fuersorge*), which for Buber is not a primordial category of life.[8] Other philosophers

---

8 Buber criticized Heidegger's *Dasein* in that it assists and helps, but does not make a person accessible to the other. Moreover, there is no perspective to mutuality in Heidegger's *Dasein*, which stays within the barriers of his own, individual being, and these barriers are not breached. In Buber's view, only a life open to another human being, in being present (*Vergegenwaertigung*), may breach these barriers. The Heideggerian solicitude or concern for the other (*Fuersorge*) does not make the other present; the other only becomes present when "one experiences the mystery of the other being in the mystery of one's own" (*im Geheimnis des eigenen Seins das Geheimnis des anderen Seins erfaehrt*). M. Buber, *Das Problem des Menschen* (Heidelberg: Lambert Schneider), pp. 106–17; idem, *Between Man and Man*, transl. Ronald Gregor Smith (New York: Macmillan, 1967), p. 170. Heidegger's openness of the self was only openness to Being, in relation with its own being, rather than the openness of a human being to his fellow human. Heidegger's man therefore remains monological,

mentioned by Jospe are Cohen and Ebner. Later studies took up the comparison between the thought of Buber and that of other thinkers. Long before Haim Gordon's comparison between Buber and Heidegger and before Rivka Horwitz's book on Buber and Ebner,[9] Eva Jospe compared these thinkers with each other.

Raphael Jospe had a good idea in thinking about the publication of his mother's MA thesis, because this study by Eva Jospe of blessed memory, which explains and discusses Buber's thought on encounter, is not only a *document humain,* testifying to the mind and heart of this admirable person, with whom I loved to talk; it remains today, five decades later, a work of academic value and interest.

---

in communication with himself, without ability to say "you." Buber unmasked Heidegger's *Dasein* as "a semblance of real life, an exalted and unblessed game of the spirit." *Das Problem,* pp, 102–103; *Between Man and Man,* p. 168.

9 Haim Gordon, "The Heidegger-Buber Controversy. The Status of the I-Thou" (*Contributions in Philosophy* 81), (Westport, Conn., London: Greenwood Press, 2001); Rivka Horwitz, *Buber's Way to 'I and Thou': The Development of Martin Buber's Thought and His 'Religion as Presence' Lectures* (see above, note 4).

# TEACHING MODERN JEWISH THOUGHT*

Having always regarded the establishment of a Jewish studies program on the American campus as desirable, I happily accepted some five or six years ago the invitation to become part of this—then still fairly new—venture. But partly because the rationale and objective of such a program seemed to me so self-evident, and partly because the experience of teaching at both The George Washington University and Georgetown University has been such an entirely positive one, I never stopped to theorize about something I considered a perfect "natural," a sort of "given." The following remarks will, subsequently, not attempt to contribute any learned theories to or scholarly analyses of the topic of Jewish education in the setting of the university. They are meant only to offer some personal reflections, observations based on pragmatic classroom situations in teaching modern Jewish thought, as well as on frequent less formal contacts with college students.

Still, even a mere practitioner of the art of teaching must proceed according to certain principles. Without them, one's choice of subject matter and methodology could hardly be determined, to say nothing of the educational goals one hopes to achieve or at least to approach. Actually, it is a somewhat artificial undertaking to describe these three—subject matter, methodology and educational goals—as distinct entities. They are, it seems to me, correlated, both functionally and substantively. One is the concomitant of the other, and all depend to a considerable degree on the teacher's personal inclinations, gifts, and aspirations.

My own field of concentration, for instance, was chosen because of my fascination with what modern Jewish thought has distilled out of classical Jewish thought. Judaism's religio-cultural tradition and its modern interpretation can, I am convinced, say much that is urgently needed to an age ("age" in the double sense of an era and of a stage in

* Originally published in *Go and Study; Essays and Studies in Honor of Alfred Jospe*, ed. Raphael Jospe and Samuel Fishman, (Washington, DC: B'nai B'rith Hillel Foundations and Ktav, 1980).

an individual's life) undergoing the stress and strain of transvaluing all values. Believing in the abiding validity of Judaism's central teachings, and touched to the core by its existential insights, I fully appreciate the various and widely varying attempts to restate these teachings and insights in an idiom apt to make them newly significant to the "new," the nineteenth and twentieth century, Jew. To be sure, not all of these attempts are ideologically acceptable or even logically compelling, and some of them, dated by their very "modernity," appear already outdated to the post-modern mind. Nevertheless, I consider their study indispensable, both as *Ding an sich* and because they build a two-way bridge between Judaism's past and future.

It is for this reason that my courses, cutting across all denominational lines without blurring any denominational distinctions, deal with the work of men (to cite only the most outstanding among numerous others) like Moses Mendelssohn, Abraham Geiger, Samson Raphael Hirsch, Leopold Zunz and Zacharias Frankel, Hermann Cohen, Leo Baeck, Franz Rosenzweig, Martin Buber, Abraham J. Heschel, and Mordecai M. Kaplan. What these and more recent representatives of modern Jewish thought have to say about certain questions with which students have either already grappled on their own, or with which they are confronted for the first time, is bound to have a direct impact upon them. I am referring to concepts (again to select but a few) such as creation, revelation, and redemption; man's freedom of will and subsequent moral responsibility; the individual's self-worth and task within society; to issues concerning the centrality of *halakhah* in Jewish life; to the tensions between faith and reason or between universalism and particularism; and to problems related to social injustice or any other kind of suffering of the innocent. A discussion of these questions can, and frequently does, reach students where they really are, so that occasionally the hoped-for happens: a mind-boggling perplexity is turned into a mind-stretching learning experience, and someone's groping progress from where he/she is to where they would like to be is helped along.

A teacher can provide another assist in that progress by showing the student how to make constructive use of the data being conveyed; that is, how to weigh and compare these frequently confusing if not contradictory nuggets of knowledge so as to integrate them into a cogently interlocking whole. Only as they learn to "see how all the pieces fall into place, how everything suddenly comes together" (as one of my seniors recently put it), will students be adequately prepared for any future academic work. The development of a faculty of intellectual discernment seems to me one of the most essential educational desiderata. The undergraduate in particular, often overwhelmed by an embarrassment of riches in the form of lectures, books, and trendy campus ideologies, needs to acquire a sense of discrimination. Without it, the student will be ill equipped to cope with any number of academic, practical, and psychological problems—among the latter, those arising from exposure to the enticements of pseudo-religious cults and life-styles euphemistically named "alternative." A student who can distinguish between open-mindedness and gullibility should be less likely to buy junk-food to satisfy what is usually referred to as "spiritual hunger," but what in reality may more often than not be merely a vague sense of disorientation and discontent.

We also discuss, of course, the historical, ideological, and psychological factors whose interaction created the *Zeitgeist* that gave rise to and fructified modern Jewish thought. Though the need for such background exploration is obvious in any case, it seems particularly urgent in the case of college students. Living almost exclusively in the present, hence existentially related only to the Now, they must be given an understanding of, and with it the possibility of relating to, the Then. To find out that and how the Now and the Then hang together in the world of ideas, and that this world did not start with anyone of us—though in a very real sense it does begin with each one of us anew—can be at once a sobering and exciting discovery.

The intellectual excitement that, fortunately, can sometimes be generated in the classroom has something to do with a notion I consider of signal importance for any kind of teaching: *relevance*. It is a notion currently not much touted about. The hue and cry for it, raised only so recently (and often so absurdly) in the halls of academe, has subsided. It has gone the way of all slogans, from deafening noise to silent discard. Yet, though my students may no longer insist on relevance, I still do. That is, I try my best to make the subject matter we are dealing with meaningful to them, to make it their personal concern, to give them a sense of *tua res agitur*. For if I succeed in making an idea come alive for them, this idea—whether disturbing or confirming some of their own notions—may give them the impetus to develop a "value-stance" (a term I borrow from Arthur Lelyveld). And this, I believe, is or ought to be the goal of any teaching which aims at being more than mere instruction, which is not satisfied merely to inform the student *of* certain values but seeks to in-form him/her *with* them.

Admittedly, I do hope to contribute to the in-forming of my students. Yet I definitely do not wish to serve as their "role-model," a function assigned to the teacher of Judaica by some writers on the subject. To assume that one does or ought to occupy a paradigmatic position is, I am afraid, conducive to assuming a pose. True, I do let my students know, in so many words or without, where I stand and what I stand for. But this stand of mine has evolved and is being maintained unalloyed by any intent to make it exemplary. In fact, the near-equation of teaching with modeling makes me acutely uncomfortable. Nevertheless, and despite my rejection of any kind of role-playing, I am far from ruling out the possibility or even likelihood that the teacher's personal convictions might exert an influence upon his/her students. I realize, moreover, that convictions and beliefs have a way of transmitting themselves, without any conscious effort on the part of those who hold them, almost osmotically—in the classroom, during personal conferences, and even over coffee and cookies in one's home, whose library or art and ceremonial objects give tangible evidence of their owner's "self-respecting rootedness in Jewish values."[1]

It is, however, precisely because I am aware of a teacher's potential for influencing students that I agree with all who consider it improper if not illegitimate to attempt any "proselytizing" in the classroom. And when that classroom is located, respectively, in a Department of Religion and a Department of Theology (as mine is), and when the courses offered stress the religio-philosophical aspect of modern Jewish thought (as mine do), this consideration is of paramount importance. There is no doubt in my mind that academic freedom, that cherished prerogative of the teacher, must extend also to the taught. My endeavor to deepen my students' understanding of modern Jewish thought is, hence, free of any conversional intent. And that goes alike for Jews and

1 Irving Greenberg, "Scholarship and Continuity: Dilemma and Dialectic"; *The Teaching of Judaica in American Universities*, p. 128.

non-Jews in my "constituency"—undergraduates, here or there interspersed with a graduate or post-graduate—whose background and diversity may (among the non-Jews) range from Muslim through American Indian to Mormon, and (among both Jews and non-Jews) from a studious religious affiliation to a studied a-religious non-affiliation.

There is, of course, no necessary connection between grasping the meaning of Judaism and embracing its faith. But even if such a connection were to exist or could be established by the teacher, the latter would be duty-bound to refrain from even the most subliminal ideological missionizing. Religious commitment, or lack thereof, must remain the student's private affair.

And yet it is not entirely correct to say that I have no conversional intent. There is a certain way in which I do wish to convert my students, though neither to Judaism if they are not Jews, nor to any of its branches if they are. I do wish to convert them in the literal sense of turning them around: from indifference to matters of the mind toward a concern with them; from a complacent acceptance of hand-me-down, preconceived notions toward investigating them; from the self-centeredness of today's "me-generation" toward a sympathetic outreach to the world. In short, I hope that their exposure to modern Jewish thought will arouse in my students an interest in thought-as-such, or that it will at least induce in them the latter's preliminary stage, thoughtfulness.

This hope of mine does not in any way contradict my just stated conviction that proselytizing and academic teaching are mutually exclusive activities. In fact, I have made this conviction a guiding principle both in presenting the various denominational approaches to Judaism to my students, and in monitoring their (actively encouraged) discussions. As for the latter, I think it mandatory that their give and take, no matter how animated, be kept free of animosity. I am trying to impress all participants—preferably by implication only, but if necessary also by explication—with the need to distinguish between convictional fervor and personal rancor, between holding an opinion and being opinionated. More than that, I should like to instill in my students respect for what Buber has called "the Other's otherness." At the moment, this is actually not particularly difficult. Ever since "doing one's own thing" (or, in a more updated version, "being into" some private, esoteric pursuit) became the dominant campus ideal, tolerance and an attitude of *laissez faire* have been the order of the day. Whether this attitude will carry over into "real" life—and in the process become a bit more selective—remains to be seen. In any event, if my students, launched on or settled in their respective careers, were to shun that internecine aggressiveness which characterizes so much of the public debate among today's professionals and scholars, one of my educational goals would be realized.

But there are other, more substantive goals to be attained, and to do so, one has to come to terms with an old pedagogical problem: the question of objectivity vs. subjectivity. Reflecting on that question (though with reference to "philosophizing" rather than teaching), Franz Rosenzweig wrote in 1927: "The obligation to be objective demands only that we look really at the entire horizon; it does not ask that we see it from a point of view other than our own, or from no particular point of view at all. Admittedly, our eyes are our eyes only; but to believe that we must pluck them out so as to see properly would bespeak a Chelmite mentality (*waere schildbuergerhaft*)."[2]

Yet it takes a wide-angle lens, an all-encompassing perspective to see the entire horizon. And the objective/subjective dilemma can become especially acute where religious convictions are involved, or in connection with so potentially loaded a question as that of early Zionist theory vs. the demands of today's *Realpolitik*, or that most haunting of subjects, the Holocaust. How evenhanded can one be in the former case, how dispassionate in the latter? Even pertaining to less soul-searing issues, one may occasionally have to tread a precariously thin line as one tries to strike a balance between objectivity and subjectivity. There is a certain ambivalence about affirming the need for academic objectivity, and at the same time feeling strongly that a teacher's job is not merely to transmit but also to evaluate data of knowledge, especially when those data have been gleaned from the fields of ideology.

The tension between objectivity and subjectivity is apparently built into the entire educational process, from the selection of one's material to its presentation, from one's methodology to its objective. And the fact

[2] Letter to Rudolf Stahl, 6/2/1927; *Briefe*, p. 597, my translation.

that all of these are, inevitably, the products of a personal pre-judgment gives rise to a dual question: how much objectivity does one owe to one's subject matter, how much subjectivity to one's students? In an effort to resolve the conflict between academic neutrality and personal value-judgment, I therefore proceed by observing the one in exploring any given issue, while expressing the other in answering any "convictional" questions put to me. In this way, I hope to do equal justice to the postulates of academic integrity and the needs of searching young minds.

The attainment of this dual objective remains an ongoing challenge. But another goal, substantively quite different and envisaged by those who originally asked that Judaica become part of the university curriculum, has by now been realized: academe's acknowledgment of Judaism's intellectual respectability. That Jewish studies have academically "arrived" is palpably noticeable in the very atmosphere in which they are pursued. There is no longer any need to engage in apologetics, nor in efforts comparable to, say, those of a Hermann Cohen, who still had to labor mightily to demonstrate that Judaism is conceptually equal to the best in Western thought. Such efforts would actually strike as undignified if not ludicrous a campus population (both faculty and students) of second and third generation American Jews—and the more so the less they realize that their own self-assurance and self-acceptance are in no small measure due to the fact that they never had to justify their own existence, nor to defend the worth and validity of their spiritual heritage.

The term spiritual heritage has become such a cliché that I am embarrassed to use it. Yet I know of no better word to describe the sum-total of that set of values, derived from the matrix of Judaism's classical sources, which modern Jewish thought examines, elucidates, or redefines. To paraphrase what I have said before: I see this examination, elucidation, or redefinition of Judaism's ethos and of its way to deal with ultimate questions not as a propagation of faith but a propagation of thought. And if the classroom is decidedly out-of-bounds for the former, it must just as decidedly become the arena for the latter. To my amazement and dismay, I often find that even seniors with their three or more years of college experience need to be coaxed to think and to question. But I also and almost invariably find that once the initial hesitation or even bewilderment have been overcome, class participation is eagerly sought and openly enjoyed.

Another source of amazement (though not of dismay) is the great difference of intellectual endowment and educational background among even a small group of students. This difference makes teaching at once harder and more of a personal challenge. I accept that challenge in something close to a fighting spirit; that is, I bend every effort to get even the less bright and least knowledgeable first interested in, and then really conversant with, our current subject, without making things tedious for the class as a whole. As for the occasional Mr. or Ms. Know-it-all-they can rather easily be shown how far they are from knowing it all. This exigency, however, arises very rarely. The great majority of my students seem genuinely receptive to what modern Jewish thought can teach them. And sometimes—joy of a teacher's joys—there are even a few who ask to be given more than the merely required reading.

Even so, I do realize that it is the need to fulfill certain degree requirements rather than an overpowering yearning for knowledge that determines most students' choice of courses. Among Jewish students, moreover (and the next few paragraphs refer to Jewish students only), there may quite possibly be some who are motivated to take a Jewish studies course by the hope that it will be a "snap." I suspect that the well-known business practice of "ethnic buying" has a campus counterpart: ethnic registering, with the negligible difference that the former is undertaken in anticipation of easy terms, and the latter in anticipation of an easy term. Should my suspicion be justified, and should among the new registrants in any course of mine really be any "ethnic" ones, they would soon find themselves disabused of the naive notion that I, by dint of being their fellow-Jew, might compromise my professional standards. Whoever enrolls in my classes is bound to realize during our first meeting that I look upon modern Jewish thought as an academic (though certainly value-oriented) discipline, and that I expect the same attitude of my students.

But there is also another, and a more acceptable, motivation for any "ethnic" course enrollment: the by now almost obligatory "search for roots" which, in turn, has something to do with the wish to establish one's self-image so as to prevent or overcome an "identity crisis." It is a motivation welcomed by some and decried by others who are concerned with these matters. I myself see nothing wrong with choosing Jewish studies as an instrumentality for finding out as much as possible about one's cultural antecedents, though I do not disregard the scholars' postulate that Judaica be studied for their own sake, as it were *by* "pure" rather than *for* any "practical" reason.

As for any identity crisis actually or potentially threatening our students—this malady, so rampant among their parents who still felt torn by the particularist/universalist conflict, seems no longer to afflict the present college generation. At least those of its members with whom I come into personal contact show no evidence of it. In fact, I see much evidence to the contrary, unless I misread the meaning of such ubiquitous badges of identification as the *kipah* on male heads (no longer worn by orthodox Jews alone) or "Jewish" ornaments around both male and female necks. Observing the campus-scene—or that minuscule and not quite typical segment of it open to my view—I gain the impression that its current Jewish residents feel entirely at ease with their Jewishness, and that somewhere along the line of succession there has been a complete transformation from Jewish self-consciousness to Jewish self-awareness. (I should add, though, that such ease need not always be a sign of affirmation. Total indifference to the fact of having been born a Jew can also make for an absence of tensions. But since those who dwell in this comfortable state for negative reasons are no likely candidates for a Jewish studies program, they are of no, or at least of no immediate, concern to our present considerations).

Strangely enough, if not paradoxically, it is the very ease with which Judaism (or, to be more precise, Jewishness) is largely accepted today which makes me somewhat uneasy. I do appreciate and indeed can enjoy the lifestyle of "doing Judaism" currently chosen by many young adults. It has a sort of folk appeal, an engaging naturalness and lively directness—all vastly preferable to the routine observance or performance of some of their elders; moreover, it is obviously emotionally satisfying to those who participate in its variegated activities. Yet spirited as these activities are, they often seem to lack a certain spirit. I mean that spirit of intellectual inquiry, indeed of soul-searching, which has at least the potential of transposing a "doing" into a "doable" Judaism, its "sancta" into its sanctification, and thus of giving to Judaism a depth dimension "doing" alone cannot bestow upon it.

A folk Judaism is doubtlessly legitimate as a cultural phenomenon, and I do not wish to derogate any of its constitutive elements. Nor do I belittle the importance of the "mood and food" factor in experiencing Judaism as a way of life. Still, a folk Judaism is, to me, not yet a full and conceptually grasped Judaism. One can surely bake a delicious challah, weave a beautiful tallit, build a sukkah and even light candles without engaging in "spiritual," let alone torturously theological, premeditations. Still, if one wishes to teach one's students that "we are responsible not for what we learn or fail to learn, but for what we think or fail to think,"[3] or if one feels that an unexamined Judaism is not worth "doing" (with due apologies to Socrates), one is happy to rediscover, and feels reassured by what Hermann Cohen, advocating "higher Jewish learning," said already in 1907: "All cultural life, including the religious, must involve the mind as well as the heart. It is not enough that our soul be satisfied and exalted by our old customs and ancient spiritual treasures. These treasures must be acquired ever anew."[4]

I am sure that the acquisition of these "treasures," along with an appreciation of the spirit which created them, remains one of the principal goals of "higher Jewish learning." I am not so sure how "high" this learning will take most of us, teachers and students alike. The plateau reached may lie all too often below the desired altitude. But as long as I am able to ascertain that my students know at the end of each semester more than they did at its start, and that they have made some small progress not only in knowledge but also in understanding, I feel that both modern Jewish thought and I, its transmitter, have fulfilled an eminently worthwhile task. For though, as I have said before, I have no wish to serve as anybody's "role-model," I do cherish the opportunity to introduce my students to that world of mind and heart and

---

3 Franz Rosenzweig, *On Jewish Learning*, Schocken Books, Inc. 1955, p. 116.

4 *Reason and Hope: Selections from the Jewish Writings of Hermann Cohen*, Translated, edited and with an Introduction by Eva Jospe. (New York: B'nai B'rith Commission on Adult Jewish Education and W.W. Norton, 1971). (Paperback edition with updated bibliography reprinted by Hebrew Union College Press, Cincinnati, 1993).

"meaning" called Judaism. It is a world of whose intrinsic value I am profoundly convinced, and to whose comprehension and perpetuation I should like to contribute my modest bit.

In conclusion, and inasmuch as these pages are written for the *Festschrift* in Alfred's honor, I want to state publicly and gratefully that it was he who originally initiated me into that world, who continues to be my personal Director of Program and Resources, though he long ago stopped being Hillel's, and without whose mentorship I might quite possibly neither have made my spiritual home in modern Jewish thought, nor have learned how to teach it.

# ENCOUNTER:

# THE THOUGHT OF MARTIN BUBER*

February 8, 1978, marked the 100th anniversary of the birth of Martin Buber, the Jewish thinker whose name has become synonymous with the terms "dialogue" and "I and Thou," and whose central ideas—far from being truly understood—have become popularized if not bowdlerized in, or by, the minds of many. With Coffee Houses being called "I and Thou," and Encounter Groups being featured attractions of Single Resorts, it seems especially important to give the thought of the foremost propounder of a philosophy of encounter its just due. The following pages constitute an attempt to trace the influences that led to the development of this philosophy, to present its premises and goals, and to give at least an indication of its validity by pointing out the principal areas to which it applies.

Martin Buber was born in Vienna in 1878 and died in Jerusalem in 1965. Since his parents were divorced when he was a very young child, he was raised in the unusually cultured household of his paternal grandparents in Lemberg, then Austrian Galicia. In addition to being a rich merchant and landowner and a secularly widely educated man, Solomon Buber was a renowned Midrash scholar. His grandson was, therefore, from early childhood on, exposed to the learned discussions of famous visitors to the Buber household. And with German, Yiddish, Hebrew and Polish spoken at home and in school, the boy grew up equally steeped in Jewish and European culture. During his university studies in Germany, Switzerland, Italy and Austria, his wide-ranging fields of concentration included languages, art and literature, politics, sociology, psychology, education, mythology, philosophy, comparative religion, and theology.

He was later to write and lecture on all of those subjects, and his output, spanning sixty years, was enormous. Yet he did not wish to

---

* Published in *JUDAISM*: A Quarterly Journal of Jewish Life and Thought, Vol. 27, No. 2, Spring Issue, 1978.

specialize in any one of these diverse fields, for he saw them all as interrelated. Actually, the term "interrelated" could almost serve as a one-word characterization of Buber's entire thought. It epitomizes his foremost concern which determined all of his thinking and his every activity: to establish relations between two or more entities that may, on the surface, seem unrelated; to create a mutuality of interests, or a meeting of minds and a sense of communality where it had not seemed likely; to achieve unity out of diversity through an encounter of, and by, the different. What he wished, therefore, to do—and what he largely succeeded in doing—was to develop a philosophical anthropology (a term borrowed from his teachers, Wilhelm Dilthey and Max Scheler), by which he meant a view of man[1] in his totality as a many-faceted yet entirely integrated human being.

Along the way to creating such an anthropological philosophy, he became, among other things, a journalist, editor and publisher, an early Zionist ideologue, and a professor of Jewish philosophy and ethics as well as of the history of religions at the University of Frankfurt/Main. In the 1920s he started to translate the Bible from Hebrew into German, a labor of love which he shared first with Franz Rosenzweig, and then continued alone after the latter's death in 1929. He completed the gigantic project thirty-two years later, in Jerusalem. With the coming of Hitler, Buber lost his position at the University in Frankfurt. But he soon became involved in reviving a singular institution that had been conceived of, and was for, a time, guided by Franz Rosenzweig, though it had not survived its founder's death: the *Freies Jüdisches Lehrhaus*, a house of intensive Jewish studies where adults pursued learning for the sake of learning, not for the sake of earning.

During this period, Buber also developed what might best be described as "consciousness-raising" resource material for adult Jewish studies, a task of immeasurable import for the shattered psyche of German Jewry, and he became instrumental in the training of teachers for Jewish schools which had to be hurriedly established after all "Aryan" schools were closed to Jewish students. He continued this spiritual rescue-work until 1938, when he emigrated to Palestine, where

1 To avoid stylistic awkwardness, "man" will be used throughout this article in generic sense and, as such encompasses woman. [E.J.]

he once again became a professor, teaching social philosophy at the Hebrew University until a few years before his death. At the same time, he wrote much for publication and went on extended lecture tours in Europe and America.

Though it was Judaism and its classical literature that nourished him throughout his life, he also synthesized in his own person and writings several other cultural sources. Both in content and style, much of his work reflects his early and profound interest in mysticism, though, in his later years, he emphatically denied being a mystic (partly because he refused, on principle, to be typecast, and partly because his personal development had taken a different direction). But he could not deny being a poet. In the Vienna of his youth, "to live meant to be immersed in art, and to think meant to be immersed in poetry" (Maringer). The effect of this total immersion stayed with him for life. Even in his most theoretical writings, Buber, the poet, occasionally gets in the way of Buber, the thinker. Moreover, his romantically complex style, at times creatively beautiful, at times badly overwritten, tends to obscure his message. The reader may become intoxicated with the mere sound of it all, or he may share the frustration of no less than a Socrates who once chided a poet for his inability to explain what he had said so beautifully.

Yet, though Buber often chooses to be poetic rather than precise, and though he surely neither was, nor probably ever wished to be, a systematic thinker, he has created a philosophy of life, something that one might almost call a "how-to" blueprint for living. This blueprint is presented largely in phenomenological terms and not as an abstractly reasoned discourse. That is, the author tends to describe some personal experience instead of offering a logical argument in support of some philosophical assertion. He may well have derived his *ad hoc,* illustrative method from Rabbinic literature and from Ḥasidic sources. For Martin Buber all but "discovered" Ḥasidism. Observing its latter-day adherents and their way of life during his boyhood in Galicia, he was so enthralled with what he saw and heard that, years later, when he was in search of spiritual roots, he returned there to study the teachings of Ḥasidism in depth, and to collect, and later translate, its rich source material for publication in the West. His findings exerted a lasting influence upon his entire outlook upon life.

These Findings have been severely criticized by Buber's erstwhile colleague at the Hebrew University, Gershom Scholem. Scholem, probably today's world-authority on Jewish mysticism and its offspring, Ḥasidism, accuses Buber of arbitrariness (if not limited knowledge) in his selections of Ḥasidic source material, and of presenting these selections in a highly one-sided and idealized manner. Worse, Scholem feels that Buber, in a "strange mixture of oversimplification, error and truth," has reshaped the Ḥasidic outlook upon life in general, and upon religious life in particular, so as to conform to his—Buber's—own. This criticism cannot be dismissed lightly by any serious student of Ḥasidism. But for us, here, it is of no immediate significance, especially since Buber himself seems to have regarded it as rather irrelevant. This, it seems, is because these two men speak a basically different language, and take a basically different approach to their work. Scholem argues as a "pure" scholar, something Buber did not claim to be, at least not in the narrowly defined way that insists on objectivity and demands impeccable attention to detail. Buber's mind reached for the stars, and was not really concerned with the tiny asterisks that must festoon the lower margin of any academically respectable page. For Scholem, Ḥasidism is a "historical phenomenon" and, as such, an object of his detached *re*search. For Buber, Ḥasidism is "the greatest phenomenon we know in the history of the spirit ... a society which lives by its faith" and, as such, it constitutes an answer to his own religious *search*.[2]

When he started out on this search as a young man, he was dissatisfied with the spiritlessness of formal religion as he knew it in the cities and among the intelligentsia of the West. At first, he was looking only for that meaning of Judaism which, he felt, lay buried somewhere in Eastern Europe, waiting to be unearthed—and to be unearthed by him. What he found surpassed his expectations. It nearly overwhelmed him in its creative richness of heart and mind, its profound insights into human nature, its emotional warmth—all indispensable elements for

2 Eventually, though, Buber came to display a more critical attitude toward this "greatest phenomenon in history," particularly vis-à-vis the "Zaddikism" (exploitation by unscrupulous "leaders") into which the movement had, in his view, here or there deteriorated.

that renewal of Judaism which he fervently sought. But he saw in Ḥasidism a significance that transcends the limits of Judaism. "Ḥasidic truth," he wrote, is, or must become, "vitally important" for all religion, and for all of life. "The Ḥasidic teaching is the proclamation of rebirth," a rebirth primarily of Judaism, but, in a larger sense, a rebirth of human spirituality. And it is in this mood and mode that Buber made himself a filter through which the accumulated wealth of Ḥasidic tales and teachings passed and, in the process, might have become both somewhat purified and somewhat less authentic.

What are these teachings, what is this spirituality, and what is Ḥasidism? Compressing the Ḥasidic world-view into the briefest possible form, and stressing only those of its aspects that seem to be reflected in the Buberian philosophy, we might answer:

Ḥasidism started as a religious and, to a large degree, mystically-oriented revival movement among eighteenth century Jews in Southern Poland and the Ukraine. The Ḥasidim set out to revive a Judaism which, they felt, had become lifeless and rigid, concerned more with formalized ritual observance of the letter than with an understanding of its original spirit. The early Ḥasidim gathered around Israel ben Eliezer, the Baal Shem Tov, who taught them to serve God with joy, in song and dance. While Judaism had traditionally almost equated piousness with learnedness, the "Besht" said that any Jew, tutored or not, can come close to God. All he needs is the right intent, an ecstatic devotion to, and a great love of, God and fellowman. *Ḥasidut* is, among other things, that religious inwardness which strives for the unification of man's external and internal life. It is a pulling together of what is seemingly—but seemingly only—apart. Reaching out to God and fellowman, I actually reach into myself; or, to put it in somewhat Buberian language, reaching out to Others, I reach myself.

Unification also means sanctification. One of Ḥasidism's central teachings that reverberates in Buber's entire philosophy—religious and secular—concerns the "hallowing of the profane" ("profane" to be understood as mundane, secular, pertaining to this-worldly matters). Actually, the Ḥasid—at least as Buber sees him—rejects the notion that there is anything profane in man's life. Whatever appears so is merely the not-as-yet-hallowed. It is up to me so to live that I sanctify, that is, fill with the right spirit, even the most trivial undertakings. If I do, my performance of even the lowliest, the most humdrum and pedestrian task will come alive with meaning. What is more, my every act, and with it my everyday life, will be not only meaningful in itself; it will represent my personal contribution to the betterment of the world. It will have a redemptive quality.

The Ḥasidic postulate for unification and sanctification, which also forms the very heart of Buber's religious thought (or, as it has lately been called, his religious secularism), is derived from a Kabbalistic myth, which relates that God, in His great love, wished to create the world. But, as the Infinite, the Limitless One, He completely filled the All. To make room for the world, He therefore withdrew Himself into Himself. This divine contraction created the possibility of an existence outside of God. The space which He had vacated contained an arrangement of vessels that were to hold the light emanating from Him. But, by some cosmic happening, the vessels broke, and the primordial light of creation spilled over. Sparks of it fell into lower spheres of being and remained there, encapsulated in all sorts of material, in constricting shells. Our earth is full of these scattered sparks. Imprisoned in their shells, they yearn to be free and to be restored to their divine source. To bring about this act of restoration, to perform this task of cosmic repair and healing, is up to me. And how do I go about it? By searching out and gathering up the dispersed sparks wherever they may be hidden. By breaking open their deadening shells so as to liberate those exiled bits of light. By performing, that is, a loving deed—my loving deed.

Looking for hidden light in even the most unlikely places and cracking the shells that encapsulate the sparks of the divine, that is what is meant by "hallowing the profane." And it is through my sanctification of the everyday, of the earthly and occasionally even the earthy, that I stitch heaven and earth together. It is through my loving deed that I hasten the redemption of the world.

Martin Buber took this bit of Kabbalistic-Ḥasidic lore and interwove it intricately with the very fabric of his philosophy. The gathering up of the sparks, for instance, and the striving for unification and restoration symbolize for him not only an ingathering of life's diverse and occasionally diametrically opposed elements; they also stand for the attempt to put together the tragically broken, the alienated Humpty Dumpties of our time, to pick up the jagged pieces of our values and our hopes which litter our personal lives as well as our interpersonal relationships, be they one-to-one, group-to-group, or international.

> "Genuine life is united life, (and for the) perfect man … all that is scattered … and fragmentary grows together in unity; this unity is his life."

Buber recognizes no division between man's animal and spiritual nature, no dichotomy between body and soul.

> "Man is not a centaur (and) [The] world is not something to be overcome. It is created reality, but reality created to be hallowed."

For Buber, the material is not immaterial, and a disembodied spirituality seems to him truly ghostly. It takes heaven and earth to make a universe, and it is the task of every individual and of society, at large, to bring about this fusion of heaven and earth, this true kingdom of God.

> He who divides his life between God and the world through giving the world "what is its," to save for God "what is His," denies God the service He demands … the hallowing of the everyday in the world and in the soul.

Yet, though our existence must not be divided into two different spheres, Buber sees all of life built on the principle of duality. Existence is not monistic. Life is grounded in a "primal twoness," a twofoldedness from which all being flows.

> If the ocean had a voice, neither high tide nor low could truly say "I," but only the two of them together in the oneness of the sea.

Similarly, neither man nor woman fully represents mankind; their differences are ineradicable. But, as human beings, they synthesize within themselves, as well as together, one with the other, their polar oppositeness; thus, they emerge complete and whole. When Buber speaks of the principle of duality which underlies all existence, he does not mean a self-destructive, self-contradictory dualism. He is well aware that, by the rules of logic, concepts such as "love and justice," "freedom and order," or even "light and darkness" do contradict each other, or even rule each other out. But he asserts that they are inseparable in the reality of lived life. Life's basic twoness manifests itself not as a struggle of irreconcilable opposites, but as a composition of constitutive elements. These elements do represent a certain polarity, but it is a polarity that neither can nor ought to be overcome. It must be lived with.

In Buber's usage, polarity or polarization means creative tension. It is a tension born not of friction but of man's recognition that there are two words by which he must live: the "primary words" I and Thou. Living by those two words, or in those two modes of existence, means that if one individual encounters an Other, he finds, or establishes, his own identity as a person, his I. I meet you and, as I discover in you the person you are, something of fundamental significance happens to both of us: we acknowledge each other's distinctiveness or selfhood. And because I become aware of my own selfhood, I can, and indeed must, affirm the selfhood of the you who faces me, and whom I face. As self encounters self, they enter into a mutual relation: they address each other as Thou.

But though I and Thou derive their being only from standing in a mutual relation with each other, their being is not relative. I and Thou are two absolutes, and must confirm each other as such. "It is from one man to another that the heavenly bread of self-being is passed." The essence of encounter lies in the realization that I and Thou are not extensions of each other. They are, and must remain, distinct personalities. Though they must give freely of themselves in the mutuality of their encounter, they must never sacrifice their individuality. Self-effacement or amorphousness of character make any real encounter impossible, for, says Buber, the "reality" of a meeting is determined by the "reality" of those who meet. A real person must be secure in the knowledge of his unique value as a human being.

Being linked to an Other in an I-Thou encounter raises the level of man's entire existence. This link is forged by performing what Buber calls the "initial act of turning," a truly life-giving motion that propels me in the direction facing you. To meet the world, to meet the Other in this world, (or the world through the Other), I must turn towards both, world and man. "Only he who turns to the other human being, and opens himself to him, receives the world in him."

Rather paradoxically, "distancing" or "setting at a distance" is as important an ingredient of encounter as is turning. Though the terms "relation" as well as "I and Thou" certainly suggest closeness, Buber insists that true closeness can arise in an encounter only when the partners understand and respect the need for a certain distance between them. A well-considered distance between any two human beings is needed if they are not to lose their very personhood.

There is, however, a vast difference between maintaining the distance which is the prerequisite for any real encounter, and keeping the kind of distance which forecloses any possibility of truly meeting another. Solitary man is not fully human. Our humanity is enhanced by, and we are the richer for, every "Thou" that we say. To say "Thou," however, is not the same as to love. Realistically considered, I cannot possibly love all of my fellowmen. Buber suggests that the Biblical commandment "Love thy neighbor as thyself' (Lev. 19:18) should be understood to mean: "Love thy neighbor as one who is like yourself." That is, I am asked to recognize in my neighbor our common humanity as precondition for entering into a dialogue with him.

What is a dialogue? In the Buberian sense, a dialogue is an attitude, a mode of life; rather than a mere conversation or exchange of views, it is a "thinking-towards-an-Other." Yet this thinking must be more than an exclusively mental or intellectual process. "We should also ... live toward the Other ... toward his person," toward his entire being. In other words, dialogical man defines neither himself nor another in purely intellectual terms. A dialogue must take into consideration the total personalities of those who are involved in it.

Dialogical man must also know how to listen, and to listen not merely to, but for, what the Other may wish to say. A real dialogue is characterized by immediacy, directness, spontaneity, non-reserve. It focuses on the common ground between the partners rather than on their differences. The components of a true dialogue are address and response; yet neither address nor response need be verbalized. Buber feels that the I's mere existence already constitutes an address, while the Thou's mere being-there constitutes a response.

Dialogical man feels himself addressed not only by another human being, but by the world and its events. The latter do not just happen. They happen to him. The drama of history is the drama of our personal lives, and its outcome depends on what we are doing with these our lives. The meaning of history is determined not by the historian but by those who live it, who are involved in it. Dialogical man experiences the world as word and must, in turn, live his entire life in response, or as a response, to that word. And as he responds to the world in all of its manifestations, he becomes responsible for it. He responds by doing, and he responds by being, willing to be both counted and accountable. He answers, as it were, life's great roll-call by calling back, affirmatively, "Here!" This "here" may at times be no more than an inarticulate stammer. We quite literally often do not know the "right" answer. In fact, there are no ready-made answers to some of the most urgent questions that life may pose. Yet, though it be tentative and fumbling, our stammering answer will be better than none. It will represent the best possible response that we can make at this particular time and in this particular situation. And, as such, it will be adequate.

Still, even an adequate response to the address of an Other—whoever or whatever that Other may be—furnishes us with no guarantee for the quality of our relationship. No human I-Thou relationship, not even the most constant one, can ever be taken for granted. It must continually be renewed from within. It must be kept mutual if it is not to degenerate into an I-It relationship.

What is the difference between I-Thou and I-It? An I-Thou encounter is characterized by mutuality. Subject faces subject (on the same level, as it were), as they reach out, one to the other, from the core of their being. By contradistinction, I-It is a subject-object relationship (reaching, as it were, from a higher to a lower level). Here, the subject tries to, or actually does, use, dominate or manipulate another person as if he were an object. This object, in turn, is passive; it does not reciprocate. The difference between an I-Thou and an I-It attitude is the difference between involvement and detachment. It has nothing to do with the distinction between animate and inanimate beings. Men can be reduced to the state of an It, while a tree, an animal, a work of art can become a Thou.

Take the example of a tree: I can look upon it as a botanical specimen, noting its generic characteristics, age and height, or maybe wonder how much fruit it might yield. In short, looking at this tree with scientific objectivity and detachment, I regard it in the mode of "It"—hence, also, as an "It." But I can, says the philosopher of encounter, also approach that tree in the attitude of "Thou," ready not only to recognize it as a being, but to enter into its very being. I shall then feel how it feels to be a tree—the upward thrust of its rough-barked trunk, the spread of its outreaching branches, the warmth of the sun dappling its leaves. What is more, by making the tree's inner "presence" present to myself, I vouchsafe the mutuality of our encounter. I activate whatever may be mutely present in the non-human "beings" whom I dialogically (that is, truly) "meet" by lending them "independence and, as it were, a soul." Thus, I will "hear" them as they call me "Thou."

Here arises, obviously, the question: how do I know that what Buber calls a dialogue is not merely my own monologue, projected onto another person? This "epistemological" problem of mine, however, is no problem of Buber's. We know because we live; we know as we live. Nor is he disturbed by the fact that this kind of knowledge is, and must remain, subjective. For is not all of existence, is not all of lived life, subjective?

Still, Martin Buber does agree that there is another, an objective kind of knowledge that is technical or scientific. Science is part of the It-world; yet it is indispensable. Buber does not advocate that we turn the clock back, ride in horse-drawn buggies, do without electricity, exchange our cities for Walden Pond. What he does suggest is that we not permit the It-world to swallow us up completely. "All real living is meeting." Man cannot live meaningfully in the dehumanizing atmosphere of It, bereft of all spirituality. Truly to live is to "live in the spirit." And to live in the spirit is to live with, and through, a Thou.

The totality of life, moreover, is infinitely greater than anything that science alone can ever comprehend. Lived life is beyond all systematization. The knowable cannot be reduced to the testable or weighable. Our approach to an understanding of reality must not be exclusively objective, logical, rational. It must be all these things, if our world is to function. But our approach to reality must be complemented by something else.

This something else is an awareness that

> the fundamental fact of human existence is man-with-man. (And when you) consider man-with-man, you see human life,

> dynamic, twofold, the giver and the receiver ... completing one another in mutual contribution.

This contribution takes many forms, but, invariably, its vehicle is communication, if only by a smile or a friendly word. Even such a negligible wisp of communication can turn into communion. And a sense of communion is the embodiment of the dialogical spirit and its ultimate goal.

But communion with the Other, even in, say, as lasting a relationship as a life-long friendship or marriage, must not lead to an attempt to make the Other over in one's own image, to change "the Other's otherness." In any real encounter, the partners' otherness must remain inviolate. This is mandatory even for antagonists, be they individuals or nations. True, ideological opponents cannot simply accept each other's views. But they can, and must, accept each other as people, and they must try to "experience the other side." To experience the other side is done most naturally in marriage, which Buber sees as the encounter *par excellence*. Marriage exemplifies the relational nature of all being and, in a unique way, can become an instrument for attaining knowledge. Life's secrets may defy solution, but, by loving, and through their love coming to know and understand another human being, husband and wife will come to know and understand the world.

Buber's view on marriage—as, indeed, on almost everything else—has stirring religious overtones. It is by our affirmation of, and sharing in, the being of the Other that we affirm, that we get a glimpse of, the being of God, that we sense His being-present to us. And it is by being answerable for one another throughout our lives that we answer "the life-long address of God."

God's address is not only life-long but world-wide, and we shall hear it anywhere, if only we will attune ourselves to it. Every individual, as well as society at large, must become "bound up in community, turned to God." Though not religious in any Orthodox sense of the term, Buber is a profoundly "religious" thinker for whom all of life must be infused with that "holy intent" which reaches outward and upward toward someone or something other than one's self—toward man, world and God (in that order). The Holy is not a realm set apart, something hovering untouchably beyond reality. The Holy is as real and touchable as the ground under our feet. Even the desert floor, seemingly yielding nothing but thornbushes, is redeemable and not only by a Moses. And even a thornbush can become the bearer of revelation-and not only to a Moses. Though the history-making revelatory events related in the Bible happened in the past, they, and revelation itself, must never become a thing of the past. Revelation is "ever present in the here and now," and any of life's multifarious manifestations can become its vehicle.

But what must we do, as individuals and collectively, to actualize the revelatory and redemptive potential of our world, this world which too often seems barren and arid? What can we do to give the body politic a soul? Society remains a lifeless construct as long as it is merely an association of individuals who live in a humanly sterile It-world. It becomes an organic structure only when we build it around the I-Thou principle. In fact, mankind's very survival depends on a reduction from the plurality of an internally unrelated composite to the singularity of a dialogically interrelated community of "human persons." Buber sees at least a hope for such a community in the kibbutz. He considers it possible to build many such "little societies" into one large, re-structured society of nations, a "community of communities" that would be bound together in the "dynamic unity of the multiform … face to face with God."

But what is to be done when "the multiform" character and ideologies of men do not permit peaceful coexistence but result in irreconcilable conflicts leading to war? Surprisingly, Buber was not an absolute pacifist. In 1939, he wrote to Gandhi:

> "I do not want force, but if there is no other way of preventing the evil from destroying the good, I trust I shall use force and give myself into God's hands."

And, nearly twenty years later, he said:

> "I do not believe that violence must always be answered with nonviolence … when there is a war, it must be fought."

These would seem to be statements not of conviction but of resignation. For the philosopher of dialogue had asked again and again that not only individuals, but also nations, live not merely next to, but truly with, one another. He had been one of the leading members of

Ihud, the organization that strove in every possible way for a unification of Arab and Jewish interests, and, for the same reason, he had joined the League of Arab and Jewish Rapprochement and Cooperation. What became of all these efforts need not be spelled out here. But it should be mentioned that Buber found himself ideologically rather isolated among his own people, especially during his later years.

This was a tragic paradox of history, for Martin Buber had been prominently associated with the Zionist movement ever since its inception. He had met Theodor Herzl already in 1898, and had entered into a close working relationship with him. But this relationship ended when Herzl's political and Buber's cultural Zionism proved incompatible. For Buber (along with Aḥad Ha-Am), this movement was infinitely more than a "nationalistically" motivated endeavor to settle Jews in Palestine. For practical reasons, it certainly had to be that, too. But though a physical haven is indispensable for the uprooted Jew, it is not enough. A land of his own is mandatory in determining the Jew's fate, but it will take more than a land of his own to fulfill the Jew's destiny as Buber sees it. Their resettlement in Palestine must make of Jews what they had always been meant to be, allowing them "to become what we are," a people imbued with the profound humanity and deep spirituality of what should be their blueprint for living: the Hebrew Bible.

With a nearly prophetic zeal, therefore, Buber implores us to work not only for Zionism but on ourselves. The Jew's task is to prepare for the rebirth, not merely of a country, but of a people; to resuscitate not merely its body politic but its soul; to revive, by a renewal from within, the ancient spirit of Israel which permeates the Bible. The Jew's task is a return to Judaism's original image of God, world and man and their interrelationship. In short, the twentieth century calls for a renascence, within Israel and without, of what Buber defines as Hebrew Humanism—a way of life that is human, humane and spiritually oriented.

"Life lived in the spirit" or "in the image of God," as he variously calls it, remains a postulate throughout Buber's writings. Yet he has no illusions about the nature of man. He recognizes the reality of evil, and even acknowledges that all societies have their "subhuman" or "contra-human" elements. This acknowledgment, however, does not invalidate his philosophy of encounter. On the contrary, it serves to underscore it. For society's "sub-humans" are evil, and create evil, precisely because they refuse to enter into any kind of dialogue with their fellowmen. To combat man-made (that is, social) evils and to reinstate its members as human beings, society needs no sweeping reforms, no slogan-promoted isms. All it needs, Buber believes, is the I-Thou spirit which creates community. And the place to start this community is here and now.

The here and now is also the place where man encounters God.

> Meet the world with the fullness of your being, and you shall meet Him … [I]f you wish to believe, love!

Though every human encounter, every loving relationship is meaningful in itself, it also points beyond itself, to a greater meaning. For the very depth with which man can experience a human encounter makes him sense the existence of an absolute presence (as indicated earlier, in connection with Buber's view on marriage). And as he realizes that it is God who has called humans into being and made them into an I, man can now turn to God, the Creator, and call Him "Thou." God is man's "eternal Thou" that, "by its nature, cannot become an It." God, the Nameless and Boundless and the eminently Other is, "paradox of paradoxes," also a Person who addresses man, and whom man can address.

God's voice can be heard through every sound of life's polyphony, not merely in synagogue, church or mosque. Buber takes a dim view of organized religion. True, religious systems and their institutions do offer man a certain sense of security but all too often they lack the sense of religious immediacy which marks a true encounter with one's Eternal Thou. "The arch of the temple-dome can easily obstruct man's view of the firmament." The Bible does not even know the word "religion," yet makes it perfectly clear how God wants man, His creature, and Israel, His people, to live. The Bible is God's dialogue with Israel. It is the classical document of I and Thou.

Though no traditionalist, Buber is not opposed to tradition as such:

> "… for without law, without some clearcut and transmissible line of demarcation between what is pleasing to God and what is displeasing to Him, there can be no historical continuity of divine rule upon earth … (Still, though) the teaching of Judaism comes

> from Sinai ... the soul of Judaism is pre- Sinaitic ... (And though) the soul can never again be understood outside of the Law ... the soul itself is not of the Law."

However—and this is a most weighty "however" indeed—Buber considers a religious law as binding upon him only if it says something to him personally, only if it assumes a compelling meaningfulness for him, only if it comes existentially alive for him. A revealed command(ment) can be meaningfully carried out only if it is experienced as a divine demand, put to, and singling out, a particular individual and claiming the entire man—his mind, will and emotion. This total seizure, as it were, burdens man with an awesome responsibility: it makes him the arbiter of truth. Yet he has no choice but to walk the "narrow ridge" in "holy insecurity," a state of mind and soul that forces him over and over again to decide what of religious tradition he can accept, and what he must reject. Even then, he will be aware that what he has decided to accept may not be *the* truth. But it will be *his* truth.

This truth constitutes the "uncertain certainty" with which "I answer for my hour." And as each man's hour and its task are inseparably intertwined with the hour and task of all other men, his personal decisions and actions determine, to a very real degree, the present shape of our society and the future of mankind. Through our decisions and actions, we become what Judaism asks us to be: creative partners of God. We become, within historical time, participants in creation, revelation and redemption, the three constitutive components of Jewish faith, the three manifestations of our Eternal Thou.

But what happens when our Eternal Thou does not become manifest to us? Where was our Divine Partner when we implored Him for a word, a sign, some response to our prayer, our outcry, in Auschwitz? To this agonized question, Buber has only an agonized answer, an answer given by Jewish tradition ever since Job: the Auschwitz of the gas-ovens, and all the other Auschwitzes throughout history, occur during an Eclipse of God. There seem to be truly God-forsaken times when, for reasons of His own, God hides His face (Deut. 31:18, 32:20, Is. 8:17, 45:15, 53:3). All man can do then is suffer silently, and silently wait for a new revealing. This suffering is not passive, however. It constitutes an act of faith: the faith that God will re-establish His presence to us, and that we shall once again "know" Him as Job "knew" Him—in the sense of serving as a witness to God's presence, which is encounterable ever anew.

There is more than a trace of mysticism in Buber's religious writings, his disavowals notwithstanding. Still, he does unconditionally reject the mystic's striving for a possible union with God. God and man can encounter each other but to encounter is not to fuse. If God and man were to become one, the principle of twoness, upon which the world rests, would be destroyed. On a different level, Buber also rejects the mystic's religious reverie. God is not to be found in some "deified" realm. The way to God leads through the world. The "fullness of time," in which the Bible places the coming of the Messiah and the world's redemption, is not some distant future. The fullness of time is now. It is the fullness of life lived in relation to, and in love of, God and man. It is life lived in the spirit. It is the life of lived and living dialogue.

# THE CONCEPT OF ENCOUNTER IN THE PHILOSOPHY OF MARTIN BUBER

## TABLE OF CONTENTS

# INTRODUCTION

Martin Buber, the foremost contemporary exponent of the philosophy of dialogue, lives in Israel as professor emeritus of the Hebrew University in Jerusalem, after decades of a creative life of writing, teaching, and lecturing. He was born in Vienna, Austria, in 1878, but spent the greater part of his childhood and adolescence in Lemberg, Galicia, where he attended the Polish *Gymnasium* while living in the house of his grandfather Solomon Buber, a distinguished Hebrew scholar and successful merchant.

In 1896, Martin Buber entered the University of Vienna to study philosophy and history of art, continuing in the same fields later at the University of Berlin. To the deep influence which Judaism as practiced, studied, and discussed in his grandfather's circle had had upon the young man was now added the stimulation of such teachers and Wilhelm Dilthey, "the founder of the history of philosophical anthropology"[1] and psychologist, and of the sociologist Georg Simmel. Buber's lifelong interest in mysticism was nourished during those years by his studies of Meister Eckhart, Nicolaus Cusanus, Paraceleus, Giordano Bruno, and Jacob Boehme.

In the cultural climate of Vienna and Berlin around the turn of the century, "Leben hiess Kunst, und Denken hiess Dichten."[2] The *Zeitgeist* which contributed to the formation of Buber's personality and thought and also to his literary style was determined to a considerable degree by the writings of the socialist theorist Gustav Landauer, by the philosopher Friedrich Nietzsche, and by such neo-romantic poets as Reiner Maria Rilke and Hugo von Hofmannsthal.

Buber was open to the mood of the time which called for a "revaluation of all values." Society, art, religion and philosophy, suffering passively and with a certain *fine-de-siècle* fatigue, the status quo of an over-intellectualizing, decadent and dying culture, were to be

---

1 Martin Buber, "What is Man!" *Between Man and Man*, trans. R.G. Smith (Boston: Beacon Press, 1957), p. 126.

2 Simon Maringer, *Martin Bubers Metaphysik der Dialogik im Zusammenhang neuerer philosophischer Strömungen, Darstellung und Kritik* (Köln: Buchdruckerei Steiner, Ulrichgasse, 1936), p. 15.

infused with a new life which would derive its impetus from the dynamics of becoming and of doing characteristic, or so it was hoped, of the spirit of a new century.

Buber saw the world as imbued with a spirit of poetry and filled with a miraculous, vital force in which he participated by the sheer intensity of his own life. He seized with equal eagerness upon the *Kulturgut* of ancient Far Eastern, of Jewish, and of European traditions, and the new ideas his contemporary world had to offer, ideas which he helped to formulate.

In 1901, he became associated with Theodor Herzl, the founder of modern Zionism, and later on with Chaim Weizmann who was to become Israel's first president. Zionism was for Buber much more than a political and nationalistic movement. Feeling himself inextricably bound to the fate of the Jews, he worked for their cultural renaissance in a land of their own, convinced that they would be able to realize their potential as God's people only in their ancient homeland Palestine.

Buber hoped that Zionism would be instrument in bringing the Jews closer to the fulfillment of what he considered their historical reality and their moral task. Their re-settlement in Palestine was to make them into what they had always been meant to be, and he was working towards this goal " ... *auf dass wir werden, was wir sind*."[3] As editor of Herzl's journal, "Die Welt," and as contributor to the publications of the "Jüdischer Verlag," Buber exerted a lasting influence upon the thinking of the intelligentsia of German speaking Jewry.

But in spite of his involvement with the Zionist movement, Buber withdrew from all official activities connected with it in 1904. For while Zionism had presented as much of a challenge and had been as personally meaningful to him as any of the ideas he was to encounter later, and while it remained of vital concern to him throughout his life, he found himself now almost overwhelmed with and absorbed by a new "discovery": *Ḥasidism.*

Ḥasidism is a religious "folk-movement" which was started some 200 years ago by Eastern European Jews in Podolia and Volhynia. As such, it seems far removed from the topic of this thesis. Yet it must be

---

3 Quoted, without source, by Hans Kohn, *Martin Buber, Sein Werk und Seine Zeit* (Köln: Melzer Verlag, 1961), p. 167.

mentioned, if only briefly, in connection with any discussion of Buber's philosophy and especially of his concept of encounter, because it played an important role in the development of both.

Ḥasidism came into being in revolt against what many Jews of the time felt to be an over-intellectual, drily legalistic attitude of rabbinic Judaism. The tendency of rabbinic Judaism to over-emphasize scholarly learning, and its insistence that God's will could be fulfilled only by following the precepts of *Halakhah*[4] down to the smallest minutiae of daily religious practice was regarded as detrimental to the development of a living and immediate relation between the common man and his God.

The Ḥasidim (the Pious Ones) were deeply religious, simple men. They felt, with a measure of naiveté and an admixture of mystic beliefs, such an inner certainty of God's living presence in their very midst that the often hair-splitting debates and the rigid formalism of "rabbinism" seemed empty and meaningless by comparison. Practicing brotherly love, they lived in communities centered around a revered and beloved teacher, the *Tsaddik*, who was personally concerned with the well-being of each of his disciples and their families, and directly accessible to them.

Love of God and love of man are central to Ḥasidic belief, putting their stamp on the Ḥasidic way of life. Though Buber discovered Ḥasidic literature only much later, he wrote that he had felt an affinity for the Ḥasidic way of life already as a boy in Lemberg where he met its latter-day adherents. They impressed him with their dual love and with their subsequent demand for the loving good deed—a love Buber has felt and a demand he has voiced throughout his life and his work.

Prayer and ritual observance play a great role in the Ḥasid's life, but he values above all man's good intention and his good deed, and the inwardness with which he sets out to "hallow" *all* of life. He embraces life in its totality, its physical as well as its spiritual aspects. For the Ḥasid knows no dichotomy between the spheres of the holy and the profane, of good and evil, or of body and soul. Buber was to express a similar view later by saying: "Man is not a centaur, he is man through

4 The body of laws regulating the life of the religiously observant Jews.

and through."[5] In fact, Buber's entire philosophy is based on the assumption that life must be lived in its concrete reality" and that this reality is composed of many layers of existence.

Ḥasidism teaches that the most exalted and the most humble are equally the work of God. The humble and even the profane many be just "shells" hiding and imprisoning the "sparks" of God's presence. It is man's glad task to break these shells by "hallowing" the profane. Hallowing means the bestowal of spiritual value on everything one does or experiences. It is to see God's ends in any and all means He may choose to carry out His Divine plan for the world and for mankind. The man who succeeds in hallowing the profane knows how to see things in their great context. For being aware of God's presence in everything, man understands that his every creaturely urge can become an instrument for serving God in joy and in grateful recognition that life in its entirety and man in his wholeness are good—the good creation of a good creator.

It is true that even the Ḥasid may at times fall short of seeing the holy in the profane, and may be plagued by "alien thoughts" which distract him momentarily from his authentic concern with the holy. But it is always within his power to turn his straying attention back, and with his heart-felt intention to return to God of whose ever-present love he can be sure.

This religious conviction found an echo in Buber, as did the attitude of a certain Tzaddik who considered his most essential concern "always just what he was engaged in at the moment."[6] Throughout his work, Buber asks for man's wholehearted concentration on and dedication to the task of the hour which, "in the immediacy of lived life"[7] is to be given priority over all other claims.

In spite of its stress on the need for inwardness, Ḥasidism does not teach withdrawal from the world. Rather than rejecting worldly concerns, the Ḥasid considers them a personal challenge which he meets

---

5 Buber, "What is Man?" *Between Man and Man,* p. 160.

6 Martin Buber, *The Origin and Meaning of Ḥasidism,* ed. and trans. M.S. Friedman (New York: Horizon Press, 1960) p. 52.

7 Martin Buber, "Productivity and Existence," *Pointing the Way,* trans. and ed. M.S. Friedman (New York: Harper and Brothers, 1957), p. 7.

by infusing them with "holiness." Affirming God's authorship of and presence in every aspect of life, the Ḥasid tries to discover the everyday world's inherent spirituality to which he responds with his own. By his piety and by his all-important good deed, he sanctifies God's name and the glory of His creation. And with a profundity of lovingness and of joyfulness he is, as Buber says in a different context (but speaking of the same attitude), "repaying living with living."[8]

Believing in the goodness, rightness and wholesomeness of life, the Ḥasid knows no existential despair. His position in the universe is marked by pride as well as by humility: in gratitude, he is certain that the world was created for man's sake; but at the same time he realizes that he is no more than dust and ashes.

However, the realization of his creatureliness does not make him cringe or grovel, for even dust and ashes are shells enclosing the Divine sparks. Hallowing the profane of his everyday life, man will become instrumental in releasing these sparks so that they may return to God's Holy Presence. In this sense, God's completeness actually depends on man's way of life—an audacious thought whose impact upon Buber is recognizable in his religious writings.

Buber spent five years collecting, examining and translating Ḥasidic legends and sayings, interpreting these "words" which represent and convey the teachings of Ḥasidism for a Western world that had, until then, been almost completely unaware of their existence. This intensive study contributed much to the gradual emergence of his world view and to the evolution of some of his most central concepts.

He shares, for instance, Ḥasidism's emphasis on "this-worldliness" which is a "holy," not a hedonistic, joy in living in the "concrete" here and now, permeated by what Buber calls "Weltgefühl."[9] And he found

---

8 *Ibid.*

9 It should be noted, however, that Ḥasidism's this-worldliness is a controversial issue among scholars. Gershom Scholem, for instance, argues (in: "Martin Bubers Deutung des Chassidismus," an article in *Literatur und Kunst, Neue Zürcher Zeitung*, Fernausgabe Nr. 142 and Nr. 2013, May 1962) that Buber's personal philosophy and his existentialism color his interpretation of Ḥasidism. Far from glorifying the here and now, Ḥasidism's approach to reality actually has Platonic overtones: hallowing the profane means to transcend the here and now. The shells of the concrete moment

in the immediacy of the Ḥasid's relation to God and to his fellow-man an anticipation of the relational thinking he was to develop later. Studying Ḥasidic legends, he said already in 1907, sixteen years before the publication of *I and Thou*: "The Legend is the myth of I and Thou, of the caller and the called, the finite which enters into the infinite and the infinite which has need of the finite."[10] Around this "myth" he created the opus of his life which consists basically of only one theme and its variations: the encounter of I and Thou.

The concept of encounter is articulated for the first time in his early work *Daniel*,[11] though the term itself is not yet used. Instead, Buber speaks of "orientation," "realization," and "direction" as characteristic attitudes in which man faces life. Orientation is the faculty for ordering and systematizing. Man orients himself in the world by sizing up his position in relation to his environment which is largely dominated by convention. But with his power of realization man fills this staked-out position with a meaning independent of convention. Realizing himself, he lives creatively out of the fullness of his own being.

In *Daniel*, Buber sees the world and mankind as a vast conglomeration of different "directions." Man, looking at the world, singles out of the infinity of countless directions which people and things take the one pointing towards himself. He matches this direction of man or thing facing him to the direction he feels to be his own, deep within himself, so that his entire being now corresponds to the being opposite him. Buber's very unusual relationship to nature which he describes repeatedly in his later works is already foreshadowed here. Seemingly under the influence of a certain cosmos-intoxication characteristic of much of his writing, he says that the man who makes the direction of a tree his own, transplants that tree from its soil into his soul, and there conceives of it as the tree of eternal life.

---

must be destroyed and the impermanence of the here and now be left behind if the Divine sparks are to be freed, that is, if permanence is to be realized in man's life.

10 Martin Buber, "Introduction," *The Legends of the Baal-Shem*, trans. M.S. Friedman (New York: Harper and Brothers, 1955), p. xiii.

11 Martin Buber, *Daniel. Gespräche von der Verwirklichung* (Leipzig: Inselverlag, 1913).

Man's relationship to other men, too, is determined by his understanding of their direction as well as of his own. Without such an insight, man's life would be a tangled web of vague possibilities, wild guesses, and non-essential involvements. But his sense of direction will assist him in seeking his own way so that he might find within himself the goal towards which to steer.[12]

The impact that the two widely divergent, "polar" fields of his interest had upon Buber, namely his academic studies and his engrossment in Ḥasidism, possibly suggested to him a theory which was to become the point of departure for all his later work: existence is not unitary and monistic; rather, it is based on a dualistic principle. He first propounded this theory in *Daniel* where he said that "the polarity of the human spirit" is an expression of the primal twoness ("die Urzwei") out of which all being flows.[13]

Buber's life and his philosophy are interrelated, the one sustaining the other. It may therefore be indicative of the state of mind he found himself in at the time that his early concept of encounter is not the meeting of man with something or someone external to himself (which it was to become later), but the tension within man himself, created by the polarity of his being.

Buber says that it has been the wisdom of the ages to recognize, and in recognition to synthesize, the duality of forces appearing under many names: mind and body, form and matter, freedom and bondage, being and becoming. Though he may be torn by the duality of his being, man can mend the rift by developing a sense of equanimity with which he counterbalances the opposing forces within himself.

Making constructive use of his inner tensions, man does not dissolve the legitimate differences of his dual nature into an indifferent mixture. Rather, he tries to bring the diverse elements of his existence together as necessary components of one unified whole. This is the unity and wholeness which a statue might sense in a marble-block out of which it

---

12 Buber makes a similar point twenty-three years later, when he writes: "'Good' is the movement in the direction of home, 'evil' in the aimless whirl of human potentialities without which nothing can be achieved and by which, if they take no direction but remain trapped in themselves, everything goes awry." "The Question to the Single One," *Between Man and Man*, p. 78.

13 Buber, "Von der Polarität," *Daniel*, p. 89ff.

was hewn.[14] If the ocean had a voice, neither high tide nor low could say I, but only the two of them together in the oneness of the whole. By the same token, neither man nor woman fully represent mankind. Their polarity is ineradicable. But as human beings, they synthesize their polar oppositeness and emerge complete and whole.

A few years after the publication of *Daniel*, Buber founded the journal *Der Jude* which he edited until 1924. This periodical voiced the conviction of Buber and other "cultural Zionists" that the interests of Jews and Arabs need not clash in Palestine. Primarily interested in the spiritual rebirth of the Jews, Buber thought their peaceful co-existence with the Arabs not only most desirable, but entirely possible. He envisioned Palestine as a bi-national state in which Arab and Jew would live together in friendship, working side by side towards the mutual goal of developing their country.

During the decade from 1923 to 1933 Buber was Professor Jewish Religion and Ethics at the University of Frankfurt am Main. At the same time he taught at the *Freies Jüdisches Lehrhaus* which had been founded there four years before as an institute of higher Jewish learning and as a forum for intellectual debates on Jewish and general religious and cultural questions. Together with Franz Rosenzweig who also taught at and at times directed the *Lehrhaus*, Buber became the personification and representative of what was best in the intellectual life of German Jews. A historically unique product of the synthesis of German and Jewish culture, the highly educated German Jew was in serious quest of spiritual values in a world which had just emerged from the traumatic experience of a war and was headed for a new crisis.

Buber and Rosenzweig became truly creative teachers of the Jewish community in Germany, interpreting the past, giving meaning to the present, and pointing the way into the future. And in addition to their *Lehrhaus*-work, they embarked on an undertaking of singular significance: they started, in 1926, their translation of the Hebrew Bible into German, a work continued by Buber alone after Rosenzweig's death in 1929, and brought to completion in March 1961. Complementing this translation, Buber has written a voluminous Bible commentary which theologians consider to be as important but also as

---

14 Buber, "Von der Einheit," *Daniel*, p. 146.

controversial as they find most of his work in the field of religious studies.[15]

If his encounter with Ḥasidism had been one of the decisive early influences upon Buber's thought, his work with the Bible became a personal encounter for him and decisively influenced his thinking during the middle period of his life. Buber sees the Hebrew Bible as *the* document of a dialogue—the dialogue between God and the children of Israel. "The basic doctrine which fills the Hebrew Bible is that our life is a dialogue between the above and the below."[16] He interprets the so-called chosenness of the Jewish people as their "vocation" in the literal sense of the word: the infinite calls, and the finite answers. It is, therefore, the historical role of the Jew to bear witness to this call by living a "holy" life as God's dialogical partner.

Discussing the dialogical nature of the Bible, Buber juxtaposes the Greek *Logos* and the Biblical *Word*. This juxtaposition serves to point out the differences between the Greek and the Hebrew approach to an understanding of truth. The Greek's way to knowledge is through his eye. He tries to grasp the truth through contemplation and through philosophical speculation hopes to arrive at a theory of first principles—all terms connected with the sense of sight. The Greek *Logos* (which is such a first principle) is static, forever and unchangeably the same. In contradistinction, the Biblical Word is dynamic, created at the moment of its utterance when it flowed in spoken language from Mount Sinai. "The Logos of the Greeks is; it has eternal being. But the Biblical Word becomes, it happens, it occurs as a spoken event."[17] The Jew's way to knowledge is through his ear. Hearing the Divine voice, he listens to the revealed truth of the "spoken event," and he answers by doing: he obeys and carries out God's spoken commandments.

---

15 Buber's religious convictions and those of Jews Orthodoxy are mutually unacceptable because of a basic disagreement about the nature and authority of religious law and its role in the life of the individual and the community.

16 Martin Buber, *At the Turning, Three Addresses on Judaism* (New York: Farrar, Straus and Young, 1952), p. 48.

17 Quoted from Martin Buber's "Biblischer Humanismus," *Der Morgen*, October 1933, by S. Meringer, *Martin Bubers Metaphysic der Dialogik*, p. 32, my translation. The same thought is very similarly expressed by Buber in *Mamre, Essays in Religion* (Melbourne and London: Melbourne U. Press, 1946), p. 4.

To Buber, the Hebrew Bible is not scripture. It is speech, and as such it is truly "The Word" of God. On the promise that the Bible must always remain speech, to be read aloud to the people (a custom still followed today in all synagogues), Buber and Rosenzweig set themselves the most difficult task: to give their German translation the word rhythm and sentence melody of the Hebrew original. When read silently, the Buber-Rosenzweig text seems unfamiliar, and the style forced. But when the words are spoken, as they are meant to be, they come alive with a strange beauty, and the linguistically almost impossible seems achieved: a Germanic language conveys and even assumes the sound of a Semitic one.

The period between the years 1933 and 1938 charged Buber with a new and grave responsibility. Conditions brought about by Hitler's régime posed particularly difficult questions concerning the general and religious education of the Jewish school population. German schools of all types were gradually closed to Jewish students, and there were neither enough non-credited Jewish schools nor qualified teachers to fill the need of these children. Moreover, the adult Jewish community, excluded from an until then rich cultural life in which it had freely participated, suffered the stunning psychological shock of sudden rejection even before it began to suffer the unspeakable agony of an almost total physical destruction. Martin Buber seemed the logical person to come to the spiritual rescue of German Jewry. As Director of the Central Office of Adult Education, he was in charge of the training of teachers for the newly established Jewish schools.

But Buber did much more than perform competently a necessary and urgent task. He became in inspiration to all those who came under his influence.

> He counseled, comforted, raised their dejected spirits. ... Perhaps not many of those who listened to him survived the fiendish slaughter, but if they perished, they died with a firmer faith in their hearts and a deeper conviction in their minds of their

> people's spiritual destiny. Martin Buber had taught them to die as Jews had always died—sanctifying the Name.[18]

Having rendered a vital service to a dying segment of world Jewry, Martin Buber now got ready to serve a segment which had just come into being. In 1938, he went to Palestine, settling in Jerusalem where he taught, until 1951, Social Philosophy at the Hebrew University. Shortly after the establishment of the State of Israel, he became the central figure in setting up a program for the training of teachers for Israel's new settlements. As the founder and co-director of an Institute for Adult Education, he worked from 1949 to 1953 towards a solution of the special educational problems which accompany the rapid influx of immigrants of widely divergent ethnic and cultural backgrounds into a new country.

Since then, Buber has been Editor-in-Chief of the Israel Encyclopedia of Education. Yet in spite of his key position in Israel's educational system, Buber is not popular with the majority of Israeli youth. It is a sad paradox that one of the earliest propounders of the Zionist idea should be rejected by the youth of the country which is largely the realization of that idea. But Buber's long years of collaboration with and his undeviating belief in the goals of *Ichud* (Union), the Association for Jewish-Arab Rapprochement (founded by the late Judah Magnes, the first president of the Hebrew University) are bitterly resented by a generation which either fought in Israel's war of independence, or which is, even today, forced to stand armed guard over its settlements on both sides of an arbitrarily drawn border-line.

Until fairly recently, Buber travelled widely, lecturing throughout Europe. He visited the United States three times between 1951 and 1958, lecturing in New York City under the sponsorship of the Jewish Theological Seminary; at the University of Michigan; in Washington, DC, in the fourth series of the William Alanson White Memorial Lectures at the School of Psychiatry; and at Princeton University as a Humanities Council Fellow.

---

18 Jacob S. Minkin, "The Amazing Martin Buber," *Congress Weekly*, XVI (January 17, 1949) p. 10ff, quoted by M.S. Friedman, *Martin Buber, the Life of Dialogue* (New York: Harper Torchbooks, Harper and Brothers, 1960), p. 266.

These lecture tours and the fact that his writings have, in rapid succession, become available to the English reader, have spread Buber's influence far beyond the comparatively small circle of his original disciples. His work is much discussed among theologians, yet it is equally stimulating to the thinking of philosophers, education, psychologists, and sociologists.

But beyond awakening the interest of scholars in several fields, Buber's ideas have a very personal appeal to his students. Listening to his lectures or reading his books, one frequently has the feeling of being addressed as an individual, drawn, as it were, into a dialogue which yields not just an intellectual but a genuinely "existential" understanding of Buber's human insights.

Transforming an anonymous public into a dialogical partner by the way in which he shares these insights, Buber becomes for his thousand-fold Thou the revered bearer of a special message. What is this message, and how does it apply to the different strata of contemporary life?

# Chapter 1

## ENCOUNTER

### I and Thou As Components of Fundamental Duality

At the core of Buber's teaching lies the message: all true life is encounter ("Alles wirkliche Leben ist Begegnung").[1] Man is not a self-sufficient entity. He does not live in a vacuum, but among multifarious other entities whose existence in some way touches his own. Realizing and affirming his interrelatedness with the world which he encounters, man enters into a dialogue with it.

The point of departure for and the culmination of this dialogue are addressing an Other as Thou. Without a Thou, he is "lost," "for in spite of his uniqueness man can never find, when he plunges to the depth of his life, a being that is whole in itself."[2] He can become whole only through relating himself to an "other." This Other is anything outside man's self: animate as well as inanimate nature, institutions as well as ideas, his fellow-man as well as God—all can constitute the Other to whom man may say Thou.

The intimacy of saying Thou sets the mood for all encounter, and imparts it with an elemental force and vitality. Buber suggests that encounter starts in the cradle. He interprets the infant's waving of arms and hands and his searching looking around as a reaching out to meet some Other. The baby stares at a red carpet, for instance, "till the soul of the red has opened itself to him," and he cuddles his teddy bear until

---

1 Martin Buber, *Ich und Du* (Leipsig: Inselverlag, 1923), p. 11. R.G. Smith in *I and Thou* (2nd ed., New York: Charles Scribner's Sons, 1958) (from which all following *I and Thou* quotations are taken), renders this sentence: "All real living is meeting." It seems, however, that encounter is a better approximation of the meaning of *Begegnung,* because the roots counter and *gegen* correspond more closely, conveying the state of being-set-over-against inherent in the German text.

2 Martin Buber, "What is Man?" *Between Man and Man,* trans. R.G. Smith (Boston: Beacon Press, 1957), p. 168.

his hands "become lovingly and unforgettably aware of its feel, texture, and shape."[3]

In the pre-conscious stage of his development, the child does not distinguish between persons and things. They are all simply colors, shapes, or sounds. But he soon grows aware that they all belong to the outside world, and he tries to pull them into his inner world. As man becomes conscious of the world external to himself as "the Other," he also becomes conscious of himself as the "I." There ensues a relationship which points into two directions: the I, encountering the Other, draws that Other towards itself, and at the same time it extends its newly discovered self in the direction of the Other.

This extension of the self towards the Other is assisted greatly by the gradual development of speech. Buber notices that man learns to say Thou (for instance in the child-mother relationship, or in primitive man's relation to Man) before he learns to say I, for his awareness of and his relation to an Other precede his awareness of his own separate existence. The Thou, Buber deduces, is innate, and it is "the a priori of relation."[4] As a human being's intellect and rationality grow, his awareness of himself develops, and his personality unfolds through an ever-increasing variety of encounters. "The inborn Thou is realised in the lived relations with that which meets it."[5] Man is the richer for every Thou he says, and the rate of his inner growth is proportional to the degree in which he relates himself to the Other as a Thou.

I and Thou are the components of life's fundamental duality (*Urzweiheit*). This duality can never be overcome. Its conscious affirmation by those who encounter each other is ontologically significant. For it is Buber's contention that an I as such has no real being. Real being is "twofold" being, rooted in and growing out of the fertile ground of an I-Thou relation. Only by saying Thou to an Other does man truly become an I.

Saying Thou to an Other transforms an ego which had until then existed in sterile isolation into an I which now will live in fruitful

---

3 Martin Buber, *I and Thou,* trans. R.G. Smith (2nd ed., New York: Charles Scribner's Sons, 1958), p. 26.

4 *Ibid.*, p. 27.

5 *Ibid.*

relation. This relation is not, or at least need not be, the same as love. Buber's request that many say Thou to his fellow-man is not a modern paraphrase of the Biblical command to love one's neighbor.[6] The Biblical command is based on the Hebrew belief in the fatherhood of God and the brotherhood of man, while Buber's request is based on his belief in the ontological character of encounter. I and Thou need not love one another; but, meeting as "Wesen und Gegenwesen," as essence confronting essence they ought to be aware that their encounter must go to the core of their being.

## 2. Knowledge by Existential Experience

Grasping the Thou's essence in mutual recognition, the I replaces the preconceptions it may have had of the Other by Other's "reality," for this until then unknown reality is now disclosed to them in their encounter. However, this disclosure, this change from unknown to known is neither the result of a closer acquaintance with, nor of a careful study of the Other. The mutual knowledge I and Thou have of each other is akin to revealed knowledge—unexplained, instantly understood, of the utmost inner lucidity and intelligibility. To know means, to Buber, to experience—not pragmatically, by using or doing, but existentially, by living.

I and Thou know each other by living each other or, to paraphrase Kierkegaard, by existing each other's existence for the duration of their encounter (which may be a moment or a lifetime). "The Thou whom I thus meet is no longer a sum of conceptions nor an object of knowledge, but a substance experienced in giving and receiving."[7]

The experience of each other's substance turns an encounter of I and Thou into an act of human comprehension in depth and in breadth. Buber says that man is as little a conglomeration of disconnected parts as melody is a conglomeration of disconnected notes. Both man and melody must be comprehended in their entirety, or they cannot be comprehended at all. When an I looks merely at one disconnected part

---

6 Lev. 19:18.

7 Martin Buber, "Bergon's Concept of Intuition," *Pointing the Way*, trans. M.S. Friedman (New York: Harper and Brothers, 1957), p. 63.

of an Other, he sees him out of context, a faceless thing to which he cannot relate himself. But a man comes truly into his own when an I looks upon him fully, with an all-comprehending glance, and calls him Thou. Witnessing this emergence of an Other's "reality" by seeing him in his true dimensions turns every I-Thou encounter into an adventure of the human spirit.

The term witnessing must not be understood in the sense of looking on, or observing. An I and a Thou are never merely passive spectators. They do not suffer from "the known sickness of modern man, who must attend his own actions as spectator."[8] I and Thou are involved in each other, wholly unselfconscious, and without vanity. They live their encounter—they do not watch it. Genuine encounter is an action, or rather an inter-action through which those who meet bear witness to each other's selfhood.

But this selfhood is very different from a mere self-reflection one might try to glimpse, narcissistically, in the mirror of an Other's personality. One would vainly search for one's own self by searching for it in an Other. Though it will be brought to its full flowering only by its relation to a Thou, the self must be firmly rooted in the I. An I merely looking for itself in an Other would find neither I nor Thou, for a self-seeking scheme is alien and fatal to the unstintingly self-giving spirit of encounter. I and Thou find each other and themselves not because they seek each Other, but because their encounter blesses them with a new understanding which is accessible only to man-in-relation.

## 3. Nature of Encounter

But when I cannot search out the Thou—how can encounter come about? "The Thou meets me through grace—it is not found by seeking."[9] Though saying Thou is "an act of my being, is indeed *the* act of my being,"[10] an I-Thou relation cannot be taken for granted, just as

8 Martin Buber, *Eclipse of God, Studies in the Relation between Religion and Philosophy* (various translators of different essays) (New York: Harper Torchbook, 1957), pp. 126–127.

9 Buber, *I and Thou*, p. 11.

10 *Ibid.*

little as life itself can be taken for granted. As life is given, so encounter is given—by grace.

However, just as life would be meaningless if men were to spend it in impassivity, waiting for divine handouts, so encounter would be meaningless unless man enlivened it by his active participation. His action lies in the perceptiveness with which he recognizes a Thou sent to him by grace, and in the way in which he addresses and activates this Thou.

When grace has brought about an encounter between man and man, they affect each other mutually: each constitutes the other's Thou. But though I and Thou have their being only through standing in a mutual relation, this being is not relative. I and Thou are two absolutes, and as such they must recognize each other. The essence of encounter lies in the realization of I and Thou that they are not each other's extension or image, but that each has a distinct personality. In spite of giving freely of themselves in the mutuality of their relation, I and Thou must not sacrifice their own individuality. They must live in accord with and true to their own natures. Amorphousness of character precludes all possibility for a real encounter, for the "reality" of a meeting is determined by the "reality" of those who meet. A *real* person must also be a real *person*, secure in the knowledge of his own human value.

Buber criticizes man's indiscriminate acceptance of any currently dominant mores with the resultant standardization of his personality just as severely as he criticizes man's making a fetish out of his own individuality out of a need to prove his being different. A real person in his straightforwardness shuns all such devices of artificiality. He has the courage to be natural, to be himself; and he shows this courage in the way he "... lives from his being."[11]

Living from one's being is inspired living. It brings out the spirit in another's being, "the actuality of the living man"[12] which is always waiting to be called upon, and to be recognized. Being recognized in the actuality of his being means to be rescued from the limitations and restrictions pedestrian, spiritless surroundings often impose upon man.

---

11 Martin Buber, "Elements of the Interhuman," trans. R.G. Smith, in *Psychiatry*, XX, No. 2 (May, 1957), p. 107.

12 Buber, "What is Man?" *Between Man and Man*, p. 163.

An encounter which grants this recognition is permeated by a certain spirituality which raises the level of man's entire existence. It gives him an inkling of the existence of an absolute to which he is linked by being linked to the Other. "In being together, the unlimited and the unconditioned is experienced."[13] Through encounter, man both gains and transcends his humanity.

Man's spiritual power affects not only his fellow-man, but it can also transform the world if he draws it into a living relation with himself. A world thus encountered is a word ensouled, converted from a chaotic mass of seemingly meaningless phenomenon into a meaningfully interrelated whole which becomes part of his own existence.

## 4. Essential Relations

Living relations between man and the world are basically different from the so-called social relations prevalent in the kind of surface-living which is marked by gregarious sociability or conventional social behavior. Relation is a category of being in Buber's philosophy, in which the position "with" assumes ontological meaning: "The fundamental fact of human existence is man with man."[14] Asserting that man's stature as a human being depends on his ability to enter into relations with others, Buber might have paraphrased Descartes' "I think, therefore I am" by saying "I stand in relation, therefore I am."

Man-with-man stands in an "essential relation" to an Other. He faces him on that level of depth where both of them really live.

> In an essential relation ... the barriers of individual being are ... breached and a new phenomenon appears which can appear only in this way: one life open to an Other ...; the Other becomes present not only in the imagination or feeling, but in the depth of one's substance, so that one experiences the mystery of the Other being in the mystery of one's own being.[15]

Such an experience illuminates the world of those who share it, and enlightens them with new insights. The warmth created in and by the

---

13 *Ibid.*, p. 168.

14 *Ibid.*, p. 203.

15 *Ibid.*, p. 170.

encounter of two essentially related human beings does not remain concentrated only upon themselves. It spreads outwards in ever widening circles even to those lives which touch their own only peripherally. Characterized by mutuality, an essential relation opens the channels running from heart to heart and makes it possible for two human beings to encounter each other in truth.

Such a true or authentic encounter is the precondition for a life of communication. A life of imparting (*Mitteilung*) is the only "real" life. Men can communicate with each other in many ways, but regardless of the form chosen, communication is basically always sharing. Sharing heightens every joy, soothes every grief, deepens all understanding. Sharing through communication adds a new dimension to all living. More than that: in Buber's view, sharing *is* living. "Where there is no sharing, there is no reality."[16]

The vehicle of this sharing is encounter. When he meets an Other, man, resolving the reserve that keeps his being apart from the Other's reaches out to make the Other's being part of his own. Through this act he gains a twofold freedom: he is liberated *from* the inauthenticity of a solitary existence, and *for* the true life of an essential or, as Buber also calls it, a creative relation.

To create is to call into being. If, as Buber says, "Creation originally means only the divine summons to the life hidden in non-being,"[17] then encounter, which is the medium for a creative relation, means a human summons to the life hidden in another being. For in a creative relation, life calls to life, and man responds to this summons by removing the mask of non-committal neutrality he wears in his every day dealings with the world.

Neutrality and objectivity have no room in a creative relation which is one of intense personal involvement and subjectivity. As men, driven and drawn to each other in encounter, submit to this mood, their innermost "substance," their hidden personality emerges: uncovering their own faces, they discover the face of the Other.

16 Buber, *I and Thou*, p. 63.

17 Buber, "Education," *Between Man and Man*, P. 84.

## 5. Primary Words

Man-in-relation epitomizes the process leading to his discovery of the true face of the Other by pronouncing "the primary word I-Thou." But man-as-spectator, uninterested in the Other's substance and refusing to share his own, observes the world as a neutral onlooker. He pronounces "the primary word I-It" in which the It can be replaced by He, She, or They.[18] I-Thou and I-It are not just words. They "are the two basic modes of our existence."[19] The primary words do not categorize the objects of relation. They characterize the nature of the relation, the two different stances man takes vis-à-vis the world. Differentiating between the two primary words does not involve a "mystical experience, but is essentially an epistemological distinction which concerns ways of perception and cognition of objects."[20]

I-Thou is not an attitude reserved exclusively for man's relation to man, nor is I-It applicable only to his relation to things. A tree may become a Thou, and a fellow human being may be treated as an It. When man stands in the attitude of Thou, he is willing to become involved. When he stands in the attitude of It, he wishes to remain detached.

The Thou-approach to life is direct and subjective, the It-approach is indirect and objective. Man may use either approach in dealing with the same object. A factory worker, for instance, operating a machine, may not ever waste a thought on it beyond keeping it in running condition. The machine is then for him a lifeless thing, an It. But if "he has understood the machine's humming as 'a merry and grateful smile ...'" in appreciation for having been repaired by him (as a worker once told Buber), he has made the machine his Thou. He has drawn a mere object "into his passionate longing for dialogue, lending it independence and as it were a soul."[21] Or when one regards the city of London as the capital of the British Empire, thinking of it in terms of population statistics or geopolitics, one uses the It-approach. But when one thinks

18 Buber, *I and Thou*, p. 3.

19 Buber, *Eclipse of God*, p. 44.

20 Z.E. Kurzweil, "Buber on Education," *Judaism*, XI, No. 1 (Winter 1962), p. 45.

21 Buber, "Dialogue," *Between Man and Man*, pp. 37–38.

of it as shrouded in luminous fog as one recalls the blurred outlines of its buildings and the vibrations of Big Ben floating through the soft air, London becomes a Thou.[22]

## 6. Encounter with Nature

By the same token, man can approach nature with the It-attitude of scientific detachment. A tree, a rock, or an animal will then be regarded as botanical, mineralogical, or zoological specimens. Man will analyze and duly catalogue their characteristics.

But he can also relate himself to nature in a most personal way, in the attitude of involvement and "intension." He then encounters tree, rock, and animal as his Thou, and they come alive for him with a living force that corresponds to the life force pulsating in him. He will understand them "as they are"—not classifiable objects, but possessing a "presence" which he can feel and absorb into his innermost being.

Buber's repeated references to I-Thou encounters with non-human beings he experienced throughout his life have led his critics to accuse him of a belief in panpsychism, and of a mysticism unbecoming a serious philosopher. But when Buber speaks of a "presence" he encounters in animate or inanimate things of nature, he adds that he does not mean to suggest that a tree has an indwelling dryad, or that rock or animal have individual souls or partake of a world-soul. A thing's "presence" means its particular being, its "So-Sein"—this tree, this rock, this animal, not just any member of a given species. And to become aware of this presence means to recognize a personal quality in that thing.

Buber's "Weltgefühl" makes him throb with the rhythm of the "élan vital" he senses all around him. "We live," he says, "our lives inscrutably included within the streaming mutual life of the universe."[23] But he does not claim to possess a mystic knowledge of the secrets of the universe. He simply says that he encounters the things of nature as they are in themselves, by concentrating all of his own being upon theirs. Their being, in turn, then discloses itself to him, to the extent that

---

22 Suggested by similar illustration by Z.E. Kurzweil, *Judaism*, XI, No. 1.

23 Buber, *I and Thou*, p. 16.

he can sense the feel a tree has of its bark as he can sense the feel he has of his own skin—not by touching either bark or skin from the outside, but by knowing them from within. Disclosing their being to him, the things of nature become his Thou.

The question of reciprocity arises here: do tree, rock, and animal, though admittedly locked in the dark sphere "beneath the level of speech"[24] have the faculty of reciprocating Buber's Thou-awareness of them? Or does he only project his own feelings into them? Is it not rather probably that Buber has lent them a life filled with his own meaning, and then has forgotten that this meaning originated with him?

Buber's answer is simple, but not conclusive: "The tree will have a consciousness, then, similar to our own? Of that I have no experience."[25]

But in spite of this stated lack of "experience" of the tree's consciousness, Buber insists that the relation between man and tree, their I-Thou encounter, is mutual, and that "no attempt be made to sap the strength from the meaning of the relation."[26] And he is quite definite in his assertion that "the tree is no impression, no lay of my imagination, no value depending on my mood; but it is bodied over against me ("er leibt mir gegenüber") and has to do with me, as I with it—only in a different way."[27]

Buber does not try to explain the different way in which the tree relates itself to him, for he does not wish to "disintegrate that which cannot be disintegrated."[28] Intellectual analysis, he seems to imply, fails to produce a comprehension of the full meaning of an "event" such as encounter. The dissecting mind disintegrates the subtly interwoven strands that go into the making of an encounter, destroying its imponderable mood.

This rejection of the possibility of a rational approach to a "happening" bordering on the irrational has been dismaying to many of Buber's students. Encouraged by his willingness to enter into a dialogue on the nature of dialogue, some of them have asked him to elucidate the

---

24 *Ibid.*, p. 6.

25 *Ibid.*, p. 8.

26 *Ibid.*

27 *Ibid.*

28 *Ibid.*

difficult problem of mutuality in an I-Thou relation between man and thing. Not wishing to "limit the dialogical relationship to those readers who made up their minds to speak," he decided "to set about giving a public answer"[29] in an attempt to clarify his position. He added a postscript to his work *I and Thou* more than forty years after it had first been published.

Unfortunately, his answer is not very satisfactory. As for an animal's reciprocating man's "saying of Thou," Buber points out that man's successful taming of animals means nothing but their manifest acceptance of "him, the stranger, in an elemental way."[30] But again he does not define what he means by the term "elemental." He only assorts that the animal's response to man's commands depends on the degree of genuineness with which he addresses them as Thou. Apart from taming animals, man can establish a close relationship to them, says Buber, if he has, in the depth of his being, "a potential partnership with animals,"[31] as well as a predominately spiritual rather than an animal nature. And while man's nature is twofold, so that his relation to an Other must be mutual by definition,[32] an animal's nature has only "a latent twofoldness." Therefore it lives on "the threshold of mutuality."[33]

This is as far as Buber's "public answer" goes, and one wonders whether the process of animal taming, accompanied as it is by the whip as well as by rewards, can in any way be described as an I-Thou encounter between tamer and tamed. It is indeed evident that domestic animals will often give signs of returning the affection lavished upon them by their masters or keepers. But it remains doubtful whether Buber is justified in calling a mutual show of affection between pet-owner and pet an I-Thou relation. Not every fondness of and liking for another being, man or animal, means necessarily a "saying of Thou." Though it may be full of warmth and friendliness, it may yet utterly lack the conscious recognition of the Other as a Thou, or the active wish

29 Buber, "Postscript to I and Thou," *I and Thou*, p. 124.

30 *Ibid.*, p. 125.

31 *Ibid.*

32 See p 14, *Supra.*

33 Buber, "Postscript to I and Thou," *I and Thou*, p. 126.

to include him or it in one's own life. But both this recognition and this active wish are basic to an I-Thou encounter.

A threshold is a line of demarcation, separating two rooms or two realms. When one lives on a threshold, as Buber says the animal does, one has not yet stepped over it. And without this stepping-over, one cannot enter the realm that lies beyond. It therefore seems impossible that an animal can reciprocate man's addressing it as Thou.

Buber's answer is still less satisfactory when he discusses the mutuality of an I-Thou relation between man and "things which come to meet us in nature."[34] He rephrases rather than clarifies his statement of forty years ago. By saying that things come to meet us he ascribes to them an ability to act by their own volition, and to behave in a certain way. Yet he admits that one cannot find "the deed or attitude of an individual being"[35] in, for instance, a plant. But in spite of this admission he does not deduce that the plant is incapable of reciprocity.

Buber feels that as long as the I who says Thou "is there," that is, as long as a man is present with his whole being, the "living wholeness and unity of the tree"[36] will be there also. The tree's being, or one might better say the being of the tree's being becomes manifest to "the sayer of Thou." The tree (as all of nature, "stretching from stones to stars" and from plants to animals) has its being in "the prethreshold or preliminal"[37] sphere. "Awakened by our attitude,"[38] that is, by our addressing things of nature as Thou, they disclose themselves to us in their essentiality. The I who approaches a tree in a Thou-attitude becomes, as it were, the tree's guarantor. He "vouchsafes" the tree's being. This vouchsafed being, this recognized "presence" of the tree constitutes its reciprocity, its response to man's address. It seems rather obvious, then, that in the sphere of preliminal mutuality the active *saying* of Thou is replaced, or symbolically represented, by the passive *being* a Thou.

---

34 *Ibid.*, pp. 124–125.

35 *Ibid.*, p. 126.

36 *Ibid.*

37 *Ibid.*

38 *Ibid.*

Preliminal mutuality differs, it would seem from true mutuality not just in degree, but in principle. For the tree's *being* a Thou will always depend on Man's vouchsafing, and can never change into an active *saying* of Thou. Man's action—his address—can never produce the tree's reaction—its response. Man may in all sincerity believe to hear the tree's voice responding to his own, but it is more likely that what he experiences subjectively as a dialogue is objectively only the echo of a monologue.

## 7. Changeability of Thou into It

As a thing of nature, lifted out of its isolated existence of neutrality and transposed into this relational world of encounter, turns from an It into a Thou, so a Thou can turn into an It by a reverse process. For encounter is not a permanent state, with I and Thou in statically fixed positions. The single encounter is a "relational event" that arises out of the fluctuating conditions which lend to a meeting—then and there, here and now, born of and frequently consummated within the moment. When this moment has passed, as invariably it must, when "the relational event has run its course,"[39] the Thou sinks back into the separated existence of neutrality, an object among objects.

This is especially true for an animal man may encounter, for the powerful grip the It-world has on it is only rarely broken by the short and delicate "appearances of the Thou."[40] When such an encounter takes place, it is like an "... almost unnoticeable sunrise and sunset of the spirit,"[41] so fleetingly brief that in most cases "... the bright Thou appeared and was gone"[42] almost before man could become fully conscious of it. The animal's "speech" in an I-Thou relation is the glance with which it "addresses" man. Thinking man, endowed with a memory, can meditate upon this glance and sustain the mood of an encounter even after this Thou has disappeared into the It-world which is its usual habitat and "burden." But the animal must sink "... back out

39 Buber, *I and Thou*, p. 33.

40 *Ibid.*, p. 98.

41 *Ibid.*

42 *Ibid.*

of the stammer of its glance into the disquietude where there is no speech and almost no memory."[43]

But not only an animal must turn back into an It. At times, a human Thou is also destined to become an It. For, says Buber, it "is the exalted melancholy of our fate that every Thou in our world must become an It."[44] This statement, taken out of contest, would be disturbing in its generalization. For though the duration and character of many relationships are indeed subject to change, not "every Thou in our world" must of necessity be a Thou only temporarily. There are many individuals who are bound to each other as I and Thou throughout their lives, for instance in marriage or in friendship. It therefore seems a safe assumption that their very constancy would make them exempt from "the exalted melancholy of our fate."

However, when Buber speaks of the impermanence of every human Thou he means something else. He compares the Thou to a butterfly which is "bound to enter the chrysalis state of the It in order to take wings anew."[45] The Thou has, as it were wings only as long as it is nourished by the mutuality of a living relationship. Lacking this life-sustaining mutuality, the Thou is turned into an It. It is spun into its cocoon of isolation, and robbed of the breath and wings of an "actual" life as it enters the dormant stage of a merely "potential" life.

Man cannot take for granted that an Other be his Thou. There is no guarantee ever for the rise of a relational event, and even less for a continuity tying one relational event to another, though man may hope for it with all his heart. For even if he himself is willing to call an Other Thou, he cannot be sure that the Other will reciprocate his feelings. The Other may be preoccupied with something else at this particular stage of his life. Therefore, he may not be attuned to the sound of the Other's Thou, and not "aware of it in the midst of his experience."[46]

Even individuals who are basically congenial may at times not be wholly synchronized in their moods, and may occasionally be insensitive to each other's needs. For, as Buber says, "... full mutuality

43 *Ibid.*
44 *Ibid.* p. 16.
45 *Ibid.*, p. 100.
46 *Ibid.*, p. 9.

is not inherent in man's life together. It is a grace, for which one must always be ready and which one never gains as an assured possession."[47]

However, in spite of the inevitable and disappointing change of a Thou into an It, due to an occasional and temporary breakdown of communication, there is hope for a re-establishment of relation and for a renewal of encounter. For the chrysalis state of It holds the promise of the eventual emergence of the butterfly Thou. But as the pupa cannot bring about its own metamorphosis, so man does not have the power, or at least is not always able to resurrect a Thou that has passed into an It. Unless "grace" lend wings to it, a living relationship may be terminated for lack of mutuality, and become a thing of the past.

## 8. Differences Between It-World and Thou-World

The past is the realm where the It exists. Man's relationship to an It is closed, a has-been. But a Thou is always encountered in the present, and man's relation to a Thou is open, a be-ing. Because the I-Thou encounter is pure present, it is irrecoverable and cannot be recounted. For by telling of an event one objectivates it, and places it into the past. ("Geschehen," as Hegel has already point out, thus becomes "Geschichte.") Moreover, encounter is so intensely personal that it must remain the private property of those who share in its intimacy. The Thou "is lived in 'a duration,'"[48] that is, internally experienced time. It is not the figment of the I's imagination but has a reality which the I experiences as a "concrete" quality. When an I encounters a Thou, the uniqueness of the one is felt and understood by the uniqueness of the Other. This singular quality of an encounter can only be apprehended, but it cannot be transmitted. The It, on the other hand, "set in the context of space and time,"[49] that is, chronological, external time, is a measurable, "abstract" quantity, and as such can become common knowledge.

There are other essential differences between the Thou-world and the It-world. The It-world is a world of ascertainable facts and figures, of

47 Buber, "Postscript to I and Thou," *I and Thou*, p. 131.

48 Buber, *I and Thou*, p. 30.

49 *Ibid*. p. 33.

scientific research, and of practical organization. It offers man the comforts of a well-regulated routine, based on practical experience and provides him with the means to earn a livelihood, and with the technical know-how that goes into the making of a civilization.

Being ruled by the laws of causality, the It-world gives man a sense of security, and of the familiar. He can rest assured in the knowledge that events will follow each other in a predictable sequence, and that certain actions will bring about certain reactions. There are few, if any independent decisions asked of man who lives in the It-world, for his course is more or less permanently mapped out for him.

The It-world with all its activities is indispensable for the progress of science and technology, and produces a "chronicle of solid benefits" for man.[50] Neither the individual nor society could survive without the props the It-world provides. "... without 'It' man cannot live, but he who lives with It alone is not a man."[51]

For man needs more than creature comforts and the security of the routinely-known. The Thou-world of relation is full of imponderables which, as each instant's new creation, are beyond the reach of research and classification. Their subtleties must be sensed and apprehended in the living experience of each moment. Every new situation facing man in the Thou-world is pregnant with a new meaning. It presents a personal challenge which must be met in an equally personal way. There are no rules of behavior by which to go, nor is it possible to predict the outcome of this new situation. In the Thou-world one cannot judge by a law of averages, for nothing is average there. The tide of life is ever-changing in its height and depth, and it is up to man to take its measure, and to base his decision upon his own findings.

In the Thou-world of free decisions we must enter, all on our own, "... into the situation which has at this moment stepped up to us, whose appearance we did not and could not know, for its like has not yet been."[52] Each man encounters life anew, and even the smallest seemingly inconsequential daily occurrence may be of consequence to

---

50 *Ibid.*, p. 34.

51 *Ibid.*

52 Buber, "Dialogue," *Between Man and Man*, p. 17.

him if he approaches it in a spirit of expectancy and takes the trouble to find out the special message it may have for him, and only for him.

To live creatively in this world, man must take upon himself the "holy insecurity" of walking "the narrow ridge."[53] In his fumbling attempt at understanding not the "how?" of the It-world but the "Why?" of the Thou-world, man gropes his way towards a hoped-for encounter in which "the last things" might be disclosed to him. In "the broad upland" of closed systems of thought men are equipped with "sure statements about the absolute."[54] But on the narrow ridge of the craggy world of the Thou no ready-made answers are to be found. Man must first struggle to find a foothold and establish a position for himself, and then he must re-think his position again and again. He must dredge up strength from his innermost resources to help him make the right decisions. For man's vista from the narrow ridge is wide; he sees open country on all sides, with no guideposts to spell out directions. In the precariousness of walking the narrow ridge lies man's freedom. "He who decides is free, for he has approached the Face."[55]

## 9. Preponderance of "It"

It is a paradox of modern life that the vast number of its intricately interdependent relationships rule out the development of more than a very few genuine relations between man and man. Modern man can no longer be on personal terms with all those whose lives, at some mostly unknown point of contact, touch his own. We hardly ever meet the people who produce, by their work, the many conveniences upon which our well-being depends to a large degree. To cut through this web of anonymity the It-world draws around us, keeping our souls isolated and imprisoned, and to open the gates into the liberating human closeness of the Thou-world is the foremost task of our time.

In our industrial society, the job has taken over the man, and the corporate function replaces the individual person. We speak, for instance, of "labor" and of "management"—not of men who carry out

53 Buber, "What is Man?" *Between Man and Man*, p. 184.

54 *Ibid.*

55 Buber, *I and Thou*, p. 51.

some given task, and of men who direct this performance. The complex machinery of an industrial society operates with statistics; there is little room or time for concern with the human needs of human beings. We are sociologically conditioned in a thousand ways—but we fail to create the one condition of real consequence for our life: the condition in which encounter can flourish.

In the unspiritual It-world of impersonal institutions, clever negotiations and perpetual busy-ness the human potential of man lies fallow. He ceases to be a genuinely human being and becomes instead a smoothly running human appliance. The It-man is typified by what has been called "the organization man" in contemporary American literature.[56] He loses sight of the goal for whose achievement the organization with which he is professionally or socially connected was founded. Instead, the organization itself becomes his main concern, replacing the direct human contact which encounter alone can provide. He becomes an efficiency expert in "human relations," but his very efficiency and expertness negate the true meaning of the term.

The organization regulates the It-man's social behavior. In his dealings with others, glibness replaces human warmth, and social poise covers up lack of human concern. He puts on an air of false heartiness, and in a show of superficial camaraderie assumes a back-slapping "hail-fellow-well-met" posture. But "well-met" is not "meeting." The well-met posture chokes the spirit of encounter which can grow only in an atmosphere of creative leisure. The It-man, however, constantly on the run, does not know creative leisure. He is harassed by a seemingly unending round of activities-for-activities'-sake, and has lost the impetus to relate himself meaningfully to an Other. He feels neither need nor inclination to say Thou.

In the depersonalized It-world men control, or use, or serve each Other. But their merely functional relationships, which are regulated by objectivity and dominated by neutrality, are devoid of all human mutuality and responsiveness, which are the hallmark of the Thou-world. The It-world is geared to economical productivity which adds materially to man's welfare. But it is unproductive of spiritual values

56 William Hollingsworth Whyte, *The Organization Man* (New York: Simon and Schuster, 1956).

and not conducive to an "authentic" human existence, that is an existence-in-relation.

Yet the It-world, though utilitarian rather than inspired, is not evil in itself. Buber does not suggest that man leave the worldliness of the It behind and retire into the seclusion of a life dedicated exclusively to the spiritual. He is convinced of the necessity and desirability of technological and scientific progress. But he warns against an over-mechanization of life and its resultant evils. He feels we are in danger of being taken over by our own inventions. Modern man, like the sorcerer's apprentice, is losing control over that which he himself called into being. We shall, says Buber, experience a "failure of the human soul"[57] if we allow our spirit to be crushed by dominion of our fearfully overgrown gadgets. He approves of the machine as long as it serves man as a tool, as an extension of his arm. But he criticizes modern man for having permitted himself to become an extension of the machine. He calls "this peculiarity of the modern crisis man's lagging behind his works."[58]

## 10. Importance of "I"

When man lags behind his works, he submits to the sovereignty of the It. Since, by definition, man can have no living, meaningful relation with an It, and relation has ontological significance as a category of being, it follows that man who lives in the It-world exclusively loses his selfhood. Having lost the faculty of saying Thou, he is no longer able to say I. But the very foundations of man's existence are anchored in the "Urzweiheit" of I and Thou.[59] It is therefore not only crucially important that man meet a Thou, but also that he be an I—a "concrete" person, an organized whole, "ein ganzer Mensch."

It is certainly neither an accident nor a mere consideration of style which prompted Buber to put the "I" first in the title of the work *I and Thou,* the by now classical statement of his philosophy of dialogue. In the "primary word I-Thou" the I is of primary importance. For without

---

57 Buber, "What is Man?" *Between Man and Man,* p. 158.

58 *Ibid.*

59 See p. 14, *Supra.*

a sincere, searching, inward concern with himself man cannot be truly concerned with the Other. A man who cannot say I, fully and with certitude, cannot say Thou either. He is a disembodied phantom. If all of life is relation, it must start out with an I which can relate itself to a Thou, or else the Thou will have no anchorage. "It is true that the child says Thou before it learns to say I, but on the height of personal existence one must be truly able to say I in order to know the mystery of the Thou in its whole truth."[60]

But there are good and bad, right and wrong ways of saying I. "The word I," Buber writes, "is the true shibboleth of mankind."[61] The way man says I characterizes his attitude towards his fellow-man and towards the world, It may be spoken by the egotist or the self-deluded, with the raspingly ugly sound of narrow and mean self-centeredness. But there also rings "the sound through the ages of the 'sufficient true and pure' saying of the I by those persons who, like Socrates and Goethe, are bound up in relation."[62] This "true and pure" I is always inclined towards the Other. Ready for encounter, it goes out to meet the world and all its creatures, and to call them Thou. The I spoken in the way Socrates and Goethe did knows no forsaken loneliness; it is the I of creative companionship, the starting point for a life of creativity.

Taking the I seriously, Buber rejects the theory, voiced, among others, by Simone Weil, that self-negation is the precondition for an ethical and religious life. He identifies himself with the view of Judaism which considers ego-centricity, selfishness, and pride grave human failings, but which affirms the unique value of the person. Without a healthy I-consciousness there can be neither Thou-consciousness nor can there be love, love of God as well as love of man. "For love does not invalidate the 'I.' ... It does not say: 'Thou art loved' but "I love thee.'"[63] And without love, there can be no ethics, nor can there be any religion.

---

60 Buber, "What is Man" *Between Man and Man*, p. 175.

61 Buber, *I and Thou*, p. 65.

62 *Ibid*., p. 66.

63 Martin Buber, "The Silent Question," in *At the Turning* (New York: Farrar, Straus and Young, 1952), p. 41.

The I that loves might be characterized as being "outerdirected," towards the Other. It is basically different from the "inner-directed" I of intellection which is bent back upon itself.[64] Buber says that

> The I in the Cartesian *ego cogito* is not the living, body-soul person whose corporality had just been disregarded by Descartes as being a matter of doubt. It is the subject of consciousness, supposedly the only function which belongs entirely to our nature. In lived concreteness ... *this* ego is not present at all. *Ego cogito* means to Descartes, indeed, not simply 'I have consciousness,' but 'It is I who have consciousness.'[65]

In Buber's view, man's awareness of himself is not the result of meditation. The Cartesian *ergo-ego,* deduced from the one undoubted certainty, cogitation, is a logical abstraction. As such, it lacks "the lived concreteness" that is the "reality" of a true I which can only be experienced existentially in the encounter with a Thou. For "not through such a deduction but only through genuine intercourse with a Thou can the I of the living person be experienced as existing."[66]

## 11. Turning

This "genuine intercourse" will become possible only after man has carried out the initial set of what Buber calls "turning." Turning is the all-important, truly life-giving movement which propels man in the direction of another man. It originates in Man's impetus to relate himself to an Other, and starts him out on the road that will eventually lead to a human encounter. Turning is a consequence of man's first realization that the individual who is locked up within himself (regardless of whether his seclusion is motivated by egoism or by an inclination to introspection) locks out the world. But "real" life must be lived in the world, in "genuine intercourse" between man and man. It is therefore essential to the very being of man that he keep the avenues of communication between himself and others open. It is Buber's recurring thesis that the individual who cuts himself off from all contact with

64 These terms were first used by David Riesman, *The Lonely Crowd* (New Haven: Yale University Press, 1950).

65 Buber, *Eclipse of God,* p. 39.

66 *Ibid.,* p. 40.

Others violates a fundamental law of life and thereby relinquishes his own claim to authentic living.

Turning, that is the execution of an about-face away from himself towards a face-to-face encounter with the Other, changes man's entire outlook upon life. As he steps into the open world of relation with its rich potential of meaning and of purpose, man's *Dasein* (existence) is transformed into *Mitsein* (co-existence; being-with-another)[67] and egoism is transformed into altruism.

But this altruism must not be mistaken for the "doing good" of official charity drives. It has nothing to do with financial generosity, nor with zealous interference in the affairs of others in the name of publicly displayed piousness. Altruism, as Buber wants it understood, means a turning towards the Other because he is the Other, and not because he is a poor unfortunate in need of being uplifted by his social, economic, or moral superior.

Turning must take place on a man's own plane of living, neither above it, nor below. It is neither an act of elevation nor of condescension. It is an act of being, performed by man who is getting ready to meet man on the level of their mutually shared and mutually fulfilled human needs.

When man, through turning, makes the Other's concerns his own, he becomes in truth his brother's keeper. His turning towards the Other expresses his willingness to assume responsibility for his fellow-man in recognition of the simple fact that they are bound to each other by their shared membership in the family of man. Buber would never consider a hermit's life, no matter how full of virtue or how rich in spiritual values, an authentically "human," "true," or "real" life. His credo that man must live a life of involvement if he wants to "live" at all might be summed up on John Donne's words:

---

67 These are Martin Heidegger's terms. See below, Ch. 4, Sec. 6, p. 121.

> No man is an Iland, intire of it selfe; every man is a peece of the Continent, a part of the maine; ... any mans death diminishes me, because I am involved in Mankinde.[68]

According to Buber, withdrawal from human involvement is akin to committing a sin—the sin of non-caring aloofness. "Original guilt consists in remaining with oneself."[69] Incapacity or unwillingness to turn towards the Other is an inexcusable human failure. It results in a severe crippling of man's faculties as a human being. The soul's full life force can be released only by its turning towards an Other. A soul which retreats into itself and becomes encapsuled within itself is, as it were, struck deaf and dumb. Unable to speak to or listen to another soul, it shrivels and wilts.

Turning towards the Other is preparatory to meeting a human being; but it is even more than that: it is a first conscious move towards a grasp of life and an apprehension of the world. For "only he who himself turns to the other human being and opens himself to him receives the world in him."[70]

---

68 John Donne, "Devotions Upon Emergent Occasions," XVI, *The Complete Poetry and Selected Prose of John Donne* (New York: The Modern Library, 1941), p. 332.

69 Buber, "What is Man" *Between Man and Man*, p. 166.

70 Buber, "Dialogue," *Between Man and Man*, p. 30.

# Chapter 2

## THE LIFE OF DIALOGUE

### 1. Dialogic

"The other human being" performs an essential function in Buber's philosophy: it complements and sustains man's state as man. Man by and for himself alone lacks true humanity. As indicated before, only man-with-man is fully a human being, in fulfillment of the basic requirement of the "Zwiefalt" of his nature. "To man, the world is twofold, in accordance with his twofold attitude."[1] There is a constant correlation not only between man and man, but also between man and the world, with man extending an eager welcome to whatever "Gestalt" the world may assume, and with the world disclosing its meaning to man's searching quest.

Man's twofold attitude finds its expression in, and takes the form of, dialogue. Buber does not make a sharp distinction in his use of the terms encounter, dialogue, dialogical life or relation, and dialogic (as noun). They are all interrelated, and partly interchangeable. An encounter is characterized by and derives its very meaning from the dialogue that grows out of it. A dialogue, in turn, cannot come about unless there is an encounter. When two or more individuals who meet in an encounter engage in or "have" a dialogue, they are "dialogically related." This dialogical relation is the activation of a latent state of heart and mind which Buber calls "dialogic."

Dialogic starts with the premise that any man and all of life is a potential dialogical partner. Dialogic is not so much the actual being engaged in a dialogue as it is the potential readiness for dialogue. It is a human quality, a willingness to draw others into the orbit of one's own life and to include them in one's thoughts and actions. Therefore it does not depend for its survival on the stimulus of the physical presence of the Other. For instance, geographically separated but dialogically

---

1 Buber, *I and Thou*, p. 3.

related individuals can and do continue "living the life of dialogue"[2] even in the absence of constant communication, as long as they maintain a sense of "that subterranean dialogic, that steady potential presence of the one to the Other"[3] which is the precondition for any dialogical relation.

Dialogic is thinking-towards the Other. Thinking-towards is not an intellectual pursuit. It is part of living-towards the Other, of "meaning" him as a person, that is, "as this personal existence"[4] whom one calls Thou. Dialogic is a mode of living, a declaration that one will accept, over and over again, life's endless offer of possible relations. "The limits of the possibilities of dialogue are the limits of awareness."[5]

The keener man's awareness, the richer his personality. Conscious of the almost inexhaustible possibilities for dialogue, man will actualize their often hidden potential in encounter after encounter. He will become what Buber calls "dialogical man." His contacts with the surrounding world will immeasurably deepen his understanding and make him grow in human stature. Dialogical man is truly "a person." As a person, he will still be subject to the inevitable fate of every creature. Yet spiritually he will transcend these limitations by reaching out from his narrowly prescribed physical realm into the metaphysical realm of encounter, dialogue and relation "which teach him the boundless continents of the boundary."[6] In this realm, man the creature becomes man the creator. For, living the life of dialogue, his impact upon others and their impact upon him create new values which are unknown to and unfelt by the man whose life, bent back upon itself in "reflexion" (*Rückbiegung*) remains a monologue.

A personal impact of man upon man can, however, not be planned, no matter how desirable it may seem. Human relations cannot be engineered, nor can dialogue be made to order. It must grow out of the immediacy of an encounter. "One cannot strive for immediacy, but one can hold oneself free and open for it. One cannot produce genuine

---

2 Buber, "Dialogue," *Between Man and Man*, p. 20.

3 Buber, "Education," *Between Man and Man*, p. 98.

4 Buber, "Elements of the Interhuman," *Psychiatry*, p. 112.

5 Buber, "Dialogue," *Between Man and Man*, p. 10.

6 *Ibid.*, p. 21.

dialogue, but one can be at its disposal."[7] An encounter must "happen" spontaneously. A pre-arranged meeting is not an encounter (though it may conceivably turn into one on occasion).

Dialogue cannot be rehearsed. A dialogically talented person is comparable to a musical one. Both can "play by ear," awakening the chords dormant in their souls and the souls of others, without having to try the effect out first. Dialogic is not a program, nor even a design for living. It is, as it were, the soul's state of alert, signifying man's preparedness to establish contact with an Other to whom he might say Thou.

## 2. Genuine and False Dialogue

Saying Thou is an expression of familiarity and closeness between men, but its true significance goes deeper than its daily usage may make apparent. Saying Thou makes a dialogue the realm of the human-ness of a human being. "... genuine dialogue is an ontological sphere which is constituted by the authenticity of being."[8]

But not all dialogue does take place in that ontological sphere. Much of what passes for dialogue entirely lacks the inwardness which is the prerequisite for those who say Thou to each other. Buber wants it understood that unless the participants of a dialogue bring to it an earnest intention to give of themselves and to share some of their own essence with the Other, the outer manifestations of their get-together may resemble a dialogue, but its inner spirit and authenticity will be missing. Small talk, polite conversation, business negotiations, intellectual discussions—all of them make use of speech and counter-speech, yet none of them are dialogues in the Buberian meaning of the term.

Buber recognizes the validity of what he calls "technical dialogue" which is an exchange of pertinent data relevant to some objective, neutral topic. As such, it is needed communication, but it remains quite outside the realm of community which alone gives rise to a genuine

7 Buber, "Prophecy, Apocalyptic, and the Historical Hour," *Pointing the Way*, p. 206.

8 Buber, "Elements of the Interhuman," *Psychiatry*, p. 112.

dialogue. In an exchange of technical information, the partners learn much about what the Other is doing, but nothing about his Being.

Technical dialogue has become the trademark of modern existence, though it has not yet completely replaced genuine dialogue. Once in a while, the aridity of our mechanized society is relieved by the sound of a human voice—maybe the train conductor's—or by the glance of an old newspaper vendor, or by the smile of a maintenance man coming to our home. These mere flashes of the dialogical spirit, illuminating the briefest of encounters, help to redeem the gracelessness Buber finds in much of present-day living.

Such a flash bears more promise for human understanding than a certain pretentious kind of dialogue which is really not a dialogue at all, but a monologue in disguise.

Buber notes that a monologue disguised as dialogue is characterized by the fact that its participants do not speak to, but at each other. Each sounds off his own opinions which are all-important to him, and neither is really interested in what the other has to say. In effect, each speaks only to himself, though the several monologues are curiously intertwined in an imitation of genuine dialogue.

Dialogically dressed-up monologue proceeds in many guises: it can take the form of a debate in which the partners aim at the weakest spot in the other armor. In the heat of the discussion man is then only intent on demolishing the other position. He disregards him totally as a person, and uses him merely as a target for his barbed remarks. Or a monological dialogue can take the form of a conversation in which the participants are not at all motivated by the wish to convince the other, let alone to understand his position. They simply need to build up their own ego by the effect they hope to have on the other.

Even friends who talk to each other may be caught in the trap of a disguised monologue. They may think of themselves and their claims for recognition as "absolute and legitimate," while they consider the Other as "relative and questionable." And it can happen that lovers, too, engage in a disguised monologue rather than in true dialogue, with each partner luxuriating in his own glorious soul and its precious sentiments, but forgetting to concentrate upon the soul of the Other.

None of these monologuists really face their partner. All of them live in a netherworld of faceless phantasms where there is no need or possibility for a genuinely dialogical encounter.

Nor can a genuine dialogue come about when men are dominated by personal vanity, or by the need to make an impression. When two such individuals meet, their conversation, says Buber ironically, actually involves "two living beings and six ghostly appearances."[9]

First, there is the one as he wishes to appear to the Other, and the Other as he wishes to appear to the one. Then there is the image each has of the Other, an image which usually does not in the least correspond to what each of them wishes the Other to see. Added to those, there is the image each has of himself. And lastly, there are the two participants in the flesh. What the six ghosts have to any mingles imperceptively with what the two individuals are saying, and a so-called dialogue is turned into a farce of which the actual participants may not even be aware in their preoccupation with themselves.

The farce develops when the occasion lacks that "climate of great faithfulness"[10] in which alone a dialogical relation can grow. Buber realizes that even dialogically related man cannot feel equally close to all men whom he encounters. There are degrees of proximity even in the life of man-with-man. But the climate of faithfulness nurtures in him a sensitivity to any possible point of contact he might have with an Other—even if it were only their "shared humanity."

A life of dialogue is a life-in-contact, though not necessarily a life of many contacts. Dialogical man does not have to deal with many people, but he must deal with people as people. He understands how to make them come alive and how to be themselves, for he himself is alive, and he is at home with himself.

Buber makes it clear that he considers dialogue primarily an attitude. It is a stance man takes, signifying his position in the world. It denotes his willingness to become (in John Dunne's words) "involved in Mankinde," and his readiness for a life of engagement and commitment. Dialogue as an attitude means availability and an openness of heart and mind to the needs and problems of others. Men

9 Buber, "Elements of the Interhuman," *Psychiatry*, p. 107.

10 *Ibid.*, p. 112.

who stand in the posture of dialogue mutually grant each other access to their innermost thoughts.

> There is genuine dialogue—no matter whether spoken or silent—where each of the participants really has in mind the Other or Others in their present and particular Being and turns to them with the intention of establishing a living mutual relation between himself and them.[11]

An actually "spoken dialogue," making use of language, must be "spoken from being to being."[12] This being is not universal being. It is the special being of this and of that man who discloses his this-ness to the Other as he speaks to him in utter sincerity and with absolute personal integrity.

Articulating the inarticulate and giving coherence to the incoherent, true dialogue interprets and in a sense re-creates the world for man. It provides him with a sense of orientation and relieves him of the anguished feeling of being lost in the universe, a cosmically displaced person.

When man, engaged in a dialogue with an Other, says Thou to him, this Thou becomes the focus for his entire world. The world and its creatures, events, thoughts, even the routinely familiar every-day happenings assume a brilliance, color and meaning they can never have for "the single one" (der Einzelne) who lives in muteness.

Dialogue not only sharpens and clarifies man's understanding of the world. Man who speaks and listens to an Other actually "receives the world in him,"[13] for within and through his perceptive grasp of the microcosm of an Other's life he perceives and grasps the macrocosm of the entire world.

Genuine dialogue never follows pre-established rules. It moves as the spirit moves its participants. It flourishes best in a climate of hospitality—a hospitality of the heart with which dialogical man invites the Other to enter his life. Genuine dialogue is characterized by the unreserved way in which men offer each other their "presence," holding back nothing that might contribute to the full value of their

---

11 Buber, "Dialogue," *Between Man and Man*, p. 19.

12 *Ibid.*, p. 20.

13 *Ibid.*, p. 30.

encounter. "... where unreserved has ruled, even wordlessly, between man, the word of dialogue has happened sacramentally."[14]

## 3. Silent Communion

Dialogue will most often be an exchange of opinion, or it will treat of some subject matter "in an objectively comprehensible form."[15] But it need not necessarily have a topic, nor need there be an actual exchange of words, though words are indeed the most frequent instruments of communication between men.

For occasionally men understand each other wordlessly. In such a moment, there occurs a "change from communication to communion."[16] Communion is, to Buber, the embodiment of the spirit of dialogue, and its ultimate goal. Communion between two kindred spirits can be so perfect that even their shared silence becomes a dialogue, as audible to them as any spoken words. Their inner rapport is so complete that the one can feel "the inclination of the head (of the Other), its injunction, as the answer to the word of your (his) silence."[17]

The shared silence enwrapping and drawing close together an I and Thou whose souls have, as it were, perfect pitch is creative, for out of it rises an enlarged capacity for understanding. Spoken words would shatter this creative silence and disturb the rare harmony of I and Thou whose inner attunement is their own form of speech. This "speech can renounce all the media of sense, and it is still speech."[18]

There is speech also in the touch or look by which lovers, friends, and members of any closely-knit group can convey their thoughts and feelings to each other. Being dialogically related, they need no verbalization to make themselves mutually understood. But, Buber points out, even strangers who have had no previous relationship can carry on a dialogue, though they neither stop to speak nor even change their pace as they pass each other on a busy street. They may do no more than exchange a smile or a glance which will "reveal to one

---

14 *Ibid.*, p. 4

15 *Ibid.*

16 *Ibid.*, p. 5

17 *Ibid.*, p. 29.

18 *Ibid.*, p. 3.

another two dialogical natures."[19] They will suddenly, if only fleetingly, find themselves united by a bond of immediate understanding. Even as they hurry off in different directions, each bent upon his own affairs, their day will have been enriched by their brief dialogical encounter.

## 4. Listening

"Dialogical natures" know not only how to speak, with words or without, but also how to listen. Horace M. Kallen once said that Renaissance man was characterized by the ability to see what he was looking at.[20] Analogically, one might say that dialogical man is characterized by the ability to listen to what he is hearing. For Renaissance man as well as for dialogical man seeing and listening are no longer exclusively functions of the sense organs. Seeing and listening become, for them, instruments of recognition and understanding. In an encounter, listening becomes interpretive hearing, an apperception of the dialogically attuned mind which goes beyond the perception of the senses.

Dialogical man who is sensitive to the needs of the Other will listen not only *to* what is actually said to him, but also *for* what is left unsaid. He will be "listening with the third ear"[21] and feel himself answerable to the unexpressed questions, doubts, and fears he detects in the Other.

The difference between listening to and listening for something may, in extreme cases, mean the difference between life and death. Buber illustrates this point by relating an episode that happened in his younger years.[22] A young man whom he did not know came to him for advice, and Buber listened to him attentively enough, and answered his questions willingly enough. The meeting took place in a friendly spirit, but without Buber's "being there in spirit." He failed to listen for the real motivation behind his visitor's questions, and therefore failed to hear the cry of despair unuttered by his guest. The young man

19 *Ibid.*, p. 5.

20 H.M. Kallen, "Dominant Ideals in Western Civilization," course given at the New School for Social Research, New York, Fall 1954.

21 Theordor Reik, *Listening With the Third Ear* (New York: Farrer, Straus, 1948).

22 Buber, "Dialogue," *Between Man and Man*, pp. 13–14.

committed suicide soon after a meeting which had not been a true encounter.

For the "truth" of an encounter and the authenticity of a dialogue are determined not only by what man says, but also by how he listens. An impaired sense of hearing in the "third" ear of dialogue impairs the quality of the dialogical relation.

Buber says that "real listening has become rare in our time."[23] He finds, especially in the field of adult education in which he has a rich experience, that today's public is more interested in the social stature of the speaker than in what he has to say. In his opinion workers, in their comparative simplicity, are better listeners than members of the middle-class, with their greater sophistication. The simpler man is still eager and willing to relate himself directly to the speaker by whom he feels himself personally addressed. But the more sophisticated "bourgeois" has largely lost the sense of immediacy that can turn a lecture into a true address.

If it is true that real listening has become rare in our time, the fault may partly lie with the speaker who all too often talks at an audience instead of speaking to his listeners. And it may be also that contemporary man's ability to listen has become deadened by the constant noise with which he surrounds himself, seemingly in a conscious or unconscious attempt to drown out the still, small voice of a potential Thou. But dialogical man knows that he must wait in receptive silence for this voice, or it will remain soundless.

Instead of cultivating our inner sense of hearing which would enable us to become better listeners to a Thou, we have become the "captive audience" of a shrill-voiced It of our own making. The "canned" music endlessly hammering away at us wherever we go on the contemporary scene may easily by symptomatic of a trend of our time to camouflage our deep-seated fear of, and ability for, being alone with ourselves, self-containedly, for any length of time. Our paucity of inner resources drives us to depend on the pseudo-companionship of a mechanized voice blaring out of an ever-present loudspeaker, rather than on the real companionship of the voice of dialogue addressing us as Thou.

---

23 Buber, *Eclipse of God*, p. 4.

The ear-splitting decibels of the It-world's incessant din, clamoring for our attention, may quite possibly have dulled not only the acuteness of our physical sense of hearing, but they may also have desensitized us psychologically to the spiritual potential of the Thou-world's dialogue. Real listening becomes indeed impossible when our attention is divided by the cacophonous shouting of the many Its surrounding us. But our faculty for listening may yet be rehabilitated by paying close attention to the "speech" of dialogue in all its multifarious possibilities.

## 5. Speech

"Speech" is for Buber anything that "says something" to man, anything capable of conveying a meaning. All of life is perpetual creation, "creation as it happens,"[24] and every happening in this on-going process is speech, addressing man. "This speech has no alphabet, each of its sounds is a new creation, and only to be grasped as such."[25] The phonetics of this speech cannot be recorded on tape, for they are ever-changing, and every listener hears and interprets the sounds differently.

Buber emphasizes that the speech of the world, "das Weltgeschehen," has no universal meaning. Listening and responding to it are an intensely personal experience which cannot be the same for any two individuals; for what "says something" to one may not say anything to another. The speech heard at any given moment by a particular man has never been heard before, and it will never be heard again in exactly the same way. It is untranslatable and untransmittable.

Yet the world's speech is neither a secret language, nor can it be understood by the select only. Each man's everyday life is full of speech, if he would only listen. "Each concrete hour ... is speech for the man who is attentive."[26]

Attentive man, not preoccupied with the selfish concerns of a drab, insular existence, becomes a reader of "signs." Signs do not appear to him in some miraculous way, nor are they supra-natural. They are to be found all around him, and it depends on his perspicacity to decipher

24 Buber, "Dialogue," *Between Man and Man*, p. 16.

25 *Ibid*.

26 *Ibid*.

their meaning. Anything man encounters, great or small, can serve as a sign announcing a dialogical potential. "Nothing can refuse to be the vessel for the Word."[27] Man therefore must be careful not to overlook a sign, for it may be the bearer of speech waiting for him to be heard. No human being one ever meets and nothing that ever happens is too insignificant for man's close attention.

Buber realizes that he may be accused of superstition for seeing signs everywhere around him. But he dismisses this possible charge by making it clear that he is not a modern "auger." An auger looks for signs and portents in the stars, in animal organs, or in cosmic events, and interprets them as having a universally applicable meaning. His so-called secret knowledge is based on ready-made rules one might as well look up in a manual: given a certain combination of circumstances or a certain constellation of occurrences, he will predict certain consequences.

But when Buber speaks of signs he means exactly the opposite: a sign is merely a signal announcing to man that here is the possibility for (not the certainty of) the development of a dialogical situation for which he should ready himself; he and no one else, and not at some future time, but now. It would indeed by superstitious, says Buber, to supercharge the events of the world with a secret meaning. But to conceive of them as one's urgent personal concern is existential belief. "The signs of address," pointing out the presence of an object for such a concern, are placed everywhere in the landscape of our existence. But we often neglect to read them, and to answer their address, out of the indolence of our hearts.

Dialogical man is not indolent. He is eagerly straining towards the sound of the world's speech. Living, to him, means to be spoken to, and the caliber of his reply is indicative of his caliber as a person. Speech becomes for him synonymous with encounter. For encounter is basically a mutual "saying something" of one to an Other. It may either be the simple "saying Thou," or it may be a complex dialogical exchange evoking a reaction of intricate thoughts, emotions, or feelings.

Man speaks with many tongues. Communicative silence, gestures, the mere being-there of dialogical man, his social action as well as his

---

27 *Ibid.*, p. 10.

artistic and intellectual creativity—any way in which one sets himself in relation to an Other—is speech for Buber. "In the house of speech are many mansions."[28]

Speech opens to man the gateway to the three spheres out of which the world of relation is built: the spheres of nature, of men, and of "spiritual beings."[29] Man's relation to nature "clings to the threshold of speech." In the sphere of nature an animal's speech consists in "the mute proclamation of the creature"[30] by which "it says something" to man; and tree or rock can similarly address him.[31]

## 6. The Sphere of Spiritual Beings. Language

The sphere of spiritual beings, which is the world of the creative human mind, is "without speech, yet begets it."[32] The world of art, for instance, "begets speech" in a twofold way: first, the artist "meets" the "form," that is an intelligible being which is waiting for him, and for him only, to be made into a work of art. By discerning the potential shape in a block of marble, the sculptor calls the form into actual being by his creative work, his "speech" which the waiting-to-be-met form "begets."

The finished sculpture can now be seen by all—and therein lies the danger of its being turned into a mere museum-piece, an object, an It. But if man who sees that sculpture (or any other artistic creation) enters into a personal relation with it and lets it speak to him, he reawakens its form and encounters it as a Thou.

The structure hidden in a work of music or art "longs as in a dream for the meeting with man, that for a timeless moment he may lift the ban and clasp the form."[33] By looking or by listening, man "meets,"

28 Buber, "Dialogue," *Between Man and Man*, p. 10.

29 This is R.G. Smith's rendition of Buber's term "geistige Wesenheiten" in *Ich und Du*. All my quotes from *I and Thou* are taken from Smith's translation. However, there is a less awkward translation of the term by M.S. Friedman: "intelligible essences."

30 Buber, *I and Thou*, pp. 101, 102

31 See "Encounter with Nature," pp. 21 ff, *Supra*.

32 Buber, *I and Thou*, p. 101.

33 *Ibid.*, p. 41.

frees, and understands the form which reveals its very essence to him as it springs to life in the responsiveness it evokes in him.

This responsiveness is man's second kind of "speech." With it, he answers the "form's silent asking,"[34] by realizing within himself the artwork's intent. Its spirit imparts itself to him and becomes his inspiration.

There seems to be a contradiction in Buber's discussion of the sphere of spiritual beings. He describes this sphere as being "without speech," yet he considers all art to be essentially dialogical. Both music and art need, so to speak, partners in order to fulfill their function. "All music calls to an ear not the musician's own."[35] And the works of painters, sculptors, and architects want to be seen by an eye other than the artist's who created them. As man listens to music or looks upon a work of art, a dialogue develops in which the genius inherent in the work "speaks" to man who responds to this disclosure with the most intense attentiveness of his soul. Rather than being "without speech," art speaks, in Buber's own definition, a unique language, and what it has to say can be expressed only in this and no other way. If this language is understood in its uniqueness by a man who is sensitive to artistic expression, it bares to him a secret but very real presence which he experiences existentially. What is thus transmitted to man in his encounter with a work of art is "not a 'feeling' but a perceived mystery."[36]

Thought, too, is dialogical, emerging out of a dynamic tension between the I and an inner Thou, an innate "genius" which confronts the "empirical self." Thinking, the I directs a question to, and receives an answer from, an indwelling spirit (Geist). It tests the validity of its thought by engaging in an inner dialogue with its "Thou-I."[37] Thought, and the work born of it, is thus a product of an encounter of the I with its Thou-I. Having been created in the internal encounter of I and Thou-I, the thought of one thinker will eventually lead to an external

---

34 *Ibid.*, p. 102.

35 Buber, "Dialogue," *Between Man and Man*, p. 25.

36 *Ibid.*

37 *Ibid.*, p. 27.

encounter with another thinker who will receive the personal message of the I, be fructified by it, and respond to it as a Thou.

For there is an undying meaningfulness in the creations of the human mind which bridge the centuries and speak to all who will listen. "Ideas are no more enthroned above our heads than resident in them; they wander amongst us and accost us,"[38] and it is up to us to translate them into our everyday reality by making them our Thou.

Historical figures and events can also become man's Thou, if he makes them come alive for him by entering into an essential relation with them. They will then communicate their true quality and "say something" to him. Resurrected from the deadness of an It-existence as a compilation of data filed away in a text-book, they will become his Thou.

In the third sphere out of which the world of relation is built, the sphere of men, relation "takes the form of speech."[39] But shifting the meaning of the term speech, Buber means in this context spoken language, consisting of conventional words. Buber assigns vital importance to language which is more than a means of communication. It is the vehicle of the "Menschenwort," the dialogical word welling up in man when he encounters an Other, and as such it is a necessary articulation of his feeling dialogically inclined towards the Other. "… I must also be intent to raise into an inner word and then into a spoken word what I have to say at this moment but do not yet possess as speech."[40]

As a link between man and man, language contributes essentially to the realization of his being, for it is instrumental in creating as well as expressing the relational "with" of the fundamental duality man-with-man. Language is consummated reciprocity, for its speech and counter-speech, exchanged by two or more individuals on the same level of consciousness, leaves no doubt as to the Other's ability to reciprocate fully. When I and Thou are actually spoken words and not only an implied attitude, they bestow upon man a reality similar to that given to man or thing by a name. As a name delivers its bearer from anonymity

38 Buber, *I and Thou*, pp. 13–14.

39 *Ibid.*, p. 101.

40 Buber, "Elements of the Interhuman," *Psychiatry*, p. 112.

and confers upon him a recognizable identity, so the pronouncing of the "objectively comprehensible" syllable Thou enhances the selfhood of an I with a new import.

## 7. Address, Response, Responsibility

For Buber, the essence of life as well as the essence of language are expressed in address and response (*Wort und Antwort*). Address and response are exemplified by the contrapuntal juxtaposition of the primary words I and Thou: The I's very existence is an address, a word, and the Thou's being-there is a response, a counter-word. The claim I and Thou have upon each other is indicative of the claim the world has upon man.

As has been shown before, dialogical man feels himself personally addressed by any of the world's events. They do not just happen. They happen to him. He experiences the world as word, and his entire life must be a counter-word.

> In our life and experience we are addressed; by thought and speech and action, by producing and influencing we are able to answer. For the most part we do not listen to the address, or we break into it with chatter. But if the word comes to us and the answer proceeds from us then human life exists, though brokenly, in the world.[41]

Life becomes truly human life when it becomes a life of responsibility. Responsibility is mans' response to a need, and an indispensable ingredient of every dialogical relation. Buber asserts that responsibility does not belong into the special province of some free-floating, disconnected ethics, out of touch with the demands of daily life. It is neither a theoretical and lofty precept, nor is it something man takes upon himself only under extra-ordinary circumstances. Responsibility must be sustained throughout the "lived life"[42] of every man, not taken on because he has occasional twinges of conscience, nor shaken off as too burdensome at some other time.

---

41 Buber, "Education," *Between Man and Man*, p. 92.

42 Buber, "Dialogue," *Ibid.*, p. 17.

Man accepts responsibility by responding to the most ordinary incidents around him, even if they were only the touch of a child's hand, or the beseeching look in a dog's eyes. Feeling responsive to, and therefore responsible for, the demands of the moment, dialogical man responds by doing, and he responds by being. Life is to him, as it were, a great roll-call which he answers by saying: "Here." This "here" of his answer may at times be no more than an inarticulate stammer, but it will be understood in its intention.

It will be an answer given "quantum satis"[43]—in a way sufficient to satisfy the demands of the hour. It may not be the fulfillment of an ideal "ought," but it will have the warmth and the human strength of a practical "can." It will be the best possible answer this man can give at this time in this situation, and as such it will be adequate, and will have validity.

In his great dialogue with life, man senses the existential need of the Other addressing him. He lives his response to this need by living responsibly, and answers the address with his full existential commitment.

The life of existential commitment is demanding and difficult, for man cannot discharge the responsibility he has taken upon himself by applying to the task of the hour a technique worked out beforehand. Any reliance on a technique or on pre-established rules would rob his response of the spontaneity and immediacy which constitute its real worth.

Man's responsibility is his alone, and consequently his response must be his alone. There is no precedent by which to gauge what his response should be, because there is no precedent to his life. Buber warns that "our age is intent on escaping from the demanding 'ever anew' of such an obligation of responsibility by a flight into a protective 'once-for-all'."[44]

Man may erect around himself fences made out of the rules and regulations of the "once-for-all." They may protect him from error, but they will also impede his immovability, and make it impossible for him to stride out freely and to meet his fellowman. His very freedom lies in

---

43 *Ibid.*, p. 38.

44 Buber, "Question," *Ibid.*, p. 70.

his realization that there are no "once-for-all" solutions, and that he will have to give his own, though untried, answers to life's "ever anew" questions and demands.

To evade this responsibility would mean to evade answering life's address which fills the Other with its "soundless thunder." We often refuse to let the sound waves of this thunder penetrate the layers of insulation we have piled up around us as a shield. For most of the time we prefer to remain undisturbed by the problems of the world, because we are afraid of the unavoidable hurts that a life of involvement must occasionally inflict upon us.

But this shirking "the obligation of responsibility" makes us unfit for the life of dialogue. For by denying an answer to the "Menschenwort" issuing from a human being, we deny him his claim to a meaningful existence. And by declining to be answerable to the world as word, we ourselves forage the possibility of a meaningful existence. Failure to accept responsibility diminishes our humanity, because it destroys the precondition for a life of relation.

## 8. Distancing

It would seem that the term relation suggests the concept of closeness. Buber makes it clear, however, that any closeness a relation might produce can come about only after the actuality of a distance between two entities has been recognized. Because of life's fundamental duality, it is imperative that the distance between the dual roots of all existence be recognized and preserved.

Awareness of the distance without which life's twofoldness would collapse is the prerequisite for entering into a relation. Life-in-relation is life-of-encounter; for in "true" life, "setting at a distance" is basic to all being.

I and Thou have their existence in being "set at a distance" from each other, and their dialogue constitutes both an affirmation and a bridging of that distance. "Distance provides the human situation, relation provides man's becoming in that situation."[45]

---

45 Martin Buber, "Distance and Relation," trans. R.G. Smith, *Psychiatry*, XX, No. 2 (May 1957), p. 100.

Buber asserts that "the primal setting at a distance"[46] is as basic a movement of human existence as is turning-towards.

As previously shown, man becomes conscious of himself as an independent being, as a self only when he learns how to differentiate between himself and Others, that is, when he becomes aware of his separate existence as one set over against an Other. To differentiate means to recognize distance. The ability to set at a distance, Buber says, marks one of the essential differences between man and animal.

An animal cannot detach itself from its surroundings. It remains forever part of its "realm," for it has no consciousness of itself as a self. Lacking this consciousness, it also has no consciousness of another as an Other. Therefore an animal cannot experience "the event of distancing,"[47] which means it has no relation to its environment except for the functional one based on its bodily needs.

But man can and does transform his "realm" into a "world," for he is aware of his separate existence. Set at a distance from the world as the Other, he simultaneously recognizes, affirms, and overcomes this distance by relating himself to the Other: "… he can accomplish the act of relation in the acknowledgement of the fundamental actuality of the distance."[48]

Buber substantiates his claim that setting at a distance is a fundamental human characteristic by pointing out the difference between a human and an insect society. Both societies assign specialized tasks to its members. But within the static insect society there exist only functional relationships necessary for its upkeep. Being unaware of the "actuality of the distance," an insect is unaware of the independent existence of another insect and therefore unable to enter into an individual relation with it.

In contradistinction, humans, being capable of "distancing," can and do cut across the boundaries of a static social system that holds its members in the bondage of a common toil. Humans enter freely into mutual relations. Their ability to set the Other at a distance releases that Other from the yoke of an indistinct mass-existence. "Distancing"

46 *Ibid.*, p. 97.

47 *Ibid.*, p. 97.

48 *Ibid.*, p. 100.

confers individuality and independence upon him and liberates him for a life of his own beyond the mere functioning as a member of a group. The dynamics of cross-relations are typical of human society, and grow out of man's conscious recognition of the distance between himself and an Other.

Tool-making, says Buber, is another manifestation of the human faculty of distancing. A monkey may force an opening in a wall with a stick it finds. But then it will drop the stick which will blend into its environment, an undistinguished object among other undistinguished objects. Man, however, sets the things he finds at hand at a distance. He recognizes their potential function, and, having put his imprint upon them by shaping them at will, he puts them aside for future use. Man's purposeful distancing has given the thing distinction by singling it out from among other things.

## 9. Otherness

Together with man's primal movement of setting the Other at a distance goes his awareness of the "otherness" of the Other. Throughout his work, Buber emphasizes the importance of accepting the inviolate otherness of the Other if a relation is to be established and maintained. For only when I and Thou accept each other as the different beings they are will they be able to contribute anything of specific value to their dialogue. "Genuine conversation, and therefore every actual fulfillment of relation between men, means acceptance of otherness."[49]

Even when, in the intimacy of encounter, soul makes contact with soul, it is a contact "with something that it is not and that it cannot become."[50] One soul cannot and should not include the Other. They must remain set over against each Other's otherness. Only when those who are dialogically related understand that they must mutually "renounce all claim to incorporating"[51] the Other can they truly call each other Thou.

49 Buber, "Distance and Relation," *Psychiatry*, p. 102.

50 Buber, *Eclipse of God*, p. 88.

51 *Ibid.*, p. 89.

The I must sense, respect, love—and leave undisturbed the otherness of the Thou. For to try and change its otherness into sameness would mean to destroy the Other, the relation, and consequently even the I which has its being only in saying Thou.

The enchantment of all true encounter lies in the deeply stirring sense of wonder at the Other's otherness. Once this sense of wonder ceases, the relation comes to an end.

As an illustration of this point Buber relates an experience he had in his early boyhood. He loved a horse his grandfather owned, and his visits to the stable were for him genuine I-Thou encounters. Stroking the horse's coat, he felt under his hand "the element of vitality itself," "... palpably the Other, not just another, really the Other itself; ..."[52] The horse, alive under his caress, was utterly different from the boy, yet related to him as his Thou. Their dialogue was shattered, though, when the boy's loving awareness of the otherness of his animal-Thou all of a sudden changed into an awareness of the pleasure his hand derived from stroking the smooth coat. Becoming conscious of touching, the boy lost touch. His dialogue with the horse turned into a monologue when the primal movement of setting at a distance was nullified by a reflexive movement of being which bent the boy's attentiveness back upon himself. He had destroyed "... the Other, the immense otherness of the Other."[53]

As previously discussed, it is absolutely essential for entering into a dialogical relation that man be aware of the otherness of the Other. This awareness depends largely on his ability to see the Other in perspective. True perspective can be gained only by setting up and maintaining a certain distance between the viewer and his object. As an object held too closely to the eye gets out of focus and becomes unrecognizable, so an individual's personality appears distorted and blurred when the distance between him and an Other is disregarded.

"Unterdistanz" (lack of distance) between man and man leads not only to a loss of perspective, but it also makes them lose their respect for the otherness of the Other, and thus undermines any dialogical relation they might have. Diminishing the vitally important distance between

52 Buber, "Dialogue," *Between Man and Man*, p. 23.

53 *Ibid.*

himself and an Other, man trespasses upon and violates the Other's most private domain, his uniqueness as a person. This violation breeds a feeling of overfamiliarity, tedium, ennui, and even contempt which makes genuine dialogue impossible.

## 10. Making Present

Yet in spite of the acknowledged necessity of setting and keeping a distance between men, encounter is meaningful only when those who meet succeed in over-arching this distance by the act of "making present" (Vergegenwärtigung). Making present means, in Buber's definition, to imagine to oneself what goes on in another person. He stresses the radical difference between imagining and having an image. An image obstructs the view of another's real self. It is an abstraction of the imagination, and as such lacks all concrete reality. But imagining is an integral part of making present, for it brings into relief the Other's being in its concrete reality—what he feels, thinks, wishes at this very moment.

Making present means seeing the Other as he is—neither as he pretends to be, nor as I want him to be. It is an act of empathy, but, as it were, in reverse: instead of putting myself into the Other's place, I bring the Other into my inner presence, holding the "living process" in him, "his very reality" before my soul. In this act of making the Other present, I "experience in the particular approximation of the given moment, the experience belonging to him as this very one."[54] My fellow-man ceases to be a component of the surrounding world which is set at a distance from me, and assumes full self-being when I "experience the Other side" in the act of making present.

Both setting at a distance (as pre-condition for establishing a relation) and making present (as establishing and "fulfilling" the closest possible relation) have, Buber says, ontological significance. For setting at a distance as "the first movement of human life puts men into mutual existence." And turning-towards, as "the second movement puts them into mutual relation."[55] First and second movements must not be

---

54 Buber, "Distance and Relation," *Psychiatry*, p. 103.

55 *Ibid.*, p. 103.

understood as following each other in temporal succession. They are independent of time and of space, and are primal ("ur"-) movements out of which the self grows.

Making present can be achieved only in an "elemental relation" between an I and a Thou who encounter each other in the dynamic center of their mutually recognized uniqueness. Mutuality is indispensable for the act of making present, "for the inmost growth of the self" and the process of "inmost self-becoming" can be accomplished only in the knowledge that both I and Thou "… have a presence in the being of the Other."[56]

Man feels an urgent need to have a presence in the Other, that is, to be confirmed by him as the being he actually is, and as the being he hopes to become. He waits hungrily for the nod of affirmation, the "Yes" from another human being, for "it is from one man to an Other that the heavenly bread of self-being is passed.[57]

## 11. Dialogue of Antagonists

Buber contends that the "yes" confirming the Other's right to his otherness must be extended even in an encounter of antagonists, or rather, that even antagonists can have a true encounter as long as they grant each Other the right to differ.

Though men may have very basic disagreements, their disputation can turn into a dialogue if it takes place in an atmosphere of mutual respect. In an encounter of opponents, each must understand that the Other's conviction stems from his very otherness which makes him see things in his own way. Still, Buber admits that one may indeed want to influence the Other. But he does not suggest any practical method by which such an influence could be exerted. He merely states emphatically that the desire to influence an Other must not result in injecting one's own "rightness" into the Other's "wrongness," nor in the attempt to change the Other basically. For an effort to make the Other over in one's own image would be equivalent to the destruction of his otherness. The only legitimate reaction to an Other's differing opinion is

56 *Ibid.*, p. 104.

57 *Ibid.*

the hope that his view of right and of truth will eventually "through my influence take seed and grow in the form suited to individuation."[58]

The process of individuation in the Other must under no circumstances be tampered with, regardless of the urgency of one's desire to convince him of the fallacy of his thought. One may feel compelled to express one's very serious opposition to the Other's conviction, but this expression must be directed at him as the person he is, in his definite being, out of which his thought has grown. Even adherents of different *Weltanschauungen* can be dialogical partners if they regard each other as fellow creatures whose confrontation must not end in a demolition of the Other's precious singular being. Acceptance of the Other's otherness is mandatory for all encounter, though acceptance need not necessarily mean approval.

There can be no dialogue if there is no "experiencing the other side," yet both sides must remain set over against each other. If one side or the other is obliterated by or absorbed in the overriding argumentativeness or overpowering personality of one of the dialogical partners, the relation is broken. An I and a Thou reach out to each other in their encounter, but their goal is a meeting, not a merging of their distinct personalities. Fusion of two personalities or subordination of the one to the other eradicates the polarity out of which dialogue arises.

There is, Buber says, a profound difference between man confronting even his opponent as a fellow-man, and an animal facing the danger with which another animal or man may threaten it. An animal "never succeeds in ascribing to the enemy an existence beyond its hostility, that is, beyond its own realm."[59] The animal, incapable of "distancing," simply suffers, fights, or seeks to escape the terrors of enmity which assume the proportions of elemental forces in its life. But man with his sense of perspective can "see the other side" of an adversary's character or of an issue he may encounter.

## 12. Seeing The Other Side

Buber is firmly convinced that it is man's duty to try and see the total personality and to encompass with his understanding the whole being

58 *Ibid.*, p. 102.

59 Buber, "Distance and Relation," *Psychiatry*, p. 102.

of the Other confronting him, though that Other may exude a spirit of animosity. For a view of all facets of his antagonist's character may actually reveal a potential Thou to the I willing and able to look for that Thou by "seeing" the Other as he is behind his concealing attitude of hostility. There is, Buber feels, always hope that "the 'bad' man, lightly touched by the holy primary word, becomes one who reveals."[60] What appears to be badness may be due largely to the partial view that the I has so far gained of the Other—partial both in the sense of being biased, and in the sense of being only part of a whole.

Inability to see the other side cripples man's potential for a dialogical encounter. A love which is "blind," for instance, which does not see the beloved in his "reality," disables man to say truly Thou; for lack of a full comprehension of an Other's nature makes an essential relation with him impossible. And hate, being blind by nature, is constitutionally unable to see, that is to understand, its object. "Yet the man who straightforwardly hates is nearer to relation than the man without hate or love,"[61] because he fulfills at least one precondition of encounter: he is passionately involved with an Other.

It is Buber's assertion that one cannot really hate a man if one knows him through and through, seeing all sides of him: "Only a part of a being can be hated."[62] Presumably he means that even a "bad" man has his good sides. It is indeed a well-known fact that even the most hardened criminal will occasionally display some good qualities. He may be fiercely loyal to his comrades, uphold unswervingly an honor-code of his own, or be generous to those for whom he cares. But does the much-documented fact of an Eichmann being a tender-hearted family-man, or of concentration camp guards lavishing loving care on a flower patch or some caged birds really make them exempt from the "wholehearted" hate by those who abhor their deeds?

Buber's answer would probably be that "he who sees a whole being and is compelled to reject it is no longer in the kingdom of hate, but is in that of human restriction of the power to say Thou."[63] The necessity of

60 Buber, *I and Thou*, p. 16.

61 *Ibid.*

62 *Ibid.*

63 *Ibid.*

having to reject an Other is not, or at least need not be, hate. It is rather a recognition of the fact that one cannot enter into an I-Thou relation with all men. For the possibility of saying Thou to an Other depends on one's willingness to accept him in his otherness, and some otherness is simply not acceptable.

As long as otherness means only differentiated being, the sum-total of all those traits that constitute an individual's personality, it must be accepted by the I whose relation to the Other as Thou is, in fact, based on this very acceptance. But there is also an otherness characterized by principles and values so vastly alien and indisputably inferior to one's own that it must be rejected as utterly unacceptable.

Buber's statements on hate and rejection, quoted above, were published in 1923. But in 1953, anguished by what he called "the crisis of man" which produced Hitler's genocide and World War II, he said:

> I, who am one of those who remained alive, have only in a formal sense a common humanity with those who took part in this action. They have so radically removed themselves from the human sphere, so transposed themselves into a sphere of monstrous inhumanity inaccessible to my conception, that not even hatred, much less an overcoming of hatred, was able to arise in me.[64]

Clearly, acceptance of the otherness of the Other and with it the possibility for dialogue is out of the question when the abyss separating man from man has eroded to such an unbridgeable depth that they must deny each other the right to call themselves human.

But as long as men do not read each other out of their shared humanity, even a clash of opinion can be permeated by a dialogical spirit. The presupposition for a dialogue between opponents is their "heartening to the human voice, ... the vox humana ..." which rings true above the wrong notes of the "contrahuman"[65] voice. Listening to that human voice, man will be reassured that it is possible to

---

64 Martin Buber, "Genuine Dialogue and the Possibilities of Peace," an address given in acceptance of the Peace Prize of the German Book Trade at Frankfurt-am-Main. Reprinted in *Pointing the Way* (New York: Harper and Brothers, 1957), p. 232.

65 *Ibid.*, p. 234.

acknowledge human distance and human otherness and yet to believe in the human Thou.

## 13. The Interhuman

Dialogue is essentially a word going back and forth between two or more individuals. It has its being in "the world of between" which provides the meeting-ground for all encounter. Man as a member of society lives in a "social realm" whose experiences and events are common to all who belong to it. Each individual existence is contained in and enclosed by a group existence, and individual and group are connected by a social relation. But dialogical man lives in an "interhuman realm" accessible only to those who stand in an essential relation with each other.

The interhuman ("das Zwischenmenschliche"), says Buber, "is a primal category of human reality" and "not an auxiliary construction."[66] It is a sphere between man and man, belonging to neither I nor Thou, but common to and mutually shared by both. It is as distinct from the individual as it is from the world, and has no continuity, but arises with each new encounter of I and Thou. A conversation, a lesson, an embrace, even a sports match—all of these are events taking place in the sphere of the Interhuman. But they must be characterized by an existential involvement which alone makes them "real," that is spontaneous to the point of mutual surprise. The deadening routine of habit falsifies and eventually destroys the true spirit of the interhuman.

Anything that happens to an individual "can be exactly distributed between the world and the soul, between an 'outer' event and an 'inner' impression."[67] But if men "happen" to each other, outer event and inner impression are transposed into a new dimension which is created by their encounter. This dimension between man and man is exclusively their own, and must not be intruded upon by an outsider.

Dialogue, in any of its genuine forms, is always a turning towards an Other. But occasionally the between-realm of the interhuman can exist even between strangers who do not face each other at all, not even in a

66 Buber, "What is Man?" *Between Man and Man*, p. 203.

67 *Ibid.*, p. 204.

symbolical sense. Buber speaks of the possibility of an "elemental dialogue" between, for instance, two strangers in a darkened concert-hall. Their dialogue is not directed at each other, but consists solely in the fact that they share the rapture of listening to music. Though their dialogical relation will vanish as soon as the lights come on again, with no carry-over into the neutral world of social relation, it was genuine in the purity and intensity of their shared experience which created a tangible if temporary bond between them.

Buber warns against explaining the dialogical situation of the between-world in psychological terms, or as mere feelings. The between-world may exist for only a few moments of a fleeting encounter, or it may be a perpetual entanglement of the irreconcilable natures of two opponents. But whatever its duration, it "can be adequately grasped only in an ontological way" as "that which has its being between them, and transcends both."[68]

The interhuman is that dimension of life in which dialogic unfolds, so that man can share the vital process (Lebensvorgang), the living event of his innermost being with an Other. It is the locality of the interplay of I and Thou through which they arrive at self-realization, becoming truly human beings. For in his dialogical relation with an Other lies man's best defense against "objectification" which strips him of his humanity as it makes him into a thing which is examined, observed, or analyzed for this or that reason. But man as a person, acting and re-acting in his concrete reality, can be perceived only in the partnership of the interhuman.

Buber says that "the essential problem of the sphere of the interhuman is the duality of being and seeming."[69] He distinguishes between two types of human existence, the one characterized by what man really is, his being; the Other by how he wishes to appear, his seeming.

In his need to find confirmation in the Other, man easily yields to the urge of "seeming." Craving the Other's approval, man puts on airs in the hope to impress the Other favorably. Buber calls man's submission to the urge of seeming his "essential cowardice." But man who lives

---

68 *Ibid.*, p. 204.

69 Buber, "Elements of the Interhuman," *Psychiatry*, p. 107.

from his "being" has "essential courage." A life lived from being is harder than a life spent in seeming, but it is worth the price. For living from one's being is authentic living, independent of meaningless conventions, and supported by confidence in the validity of one's own standards.

Genuine dialogue, as has been shown before, depends on the "being," that is the genuineness of its participants.

It cannot come about when men pretend to be what they are not, or when they show each other a façade instead of a face. A scheme calculated to create an effect upon an Other invalidates a dialogical relation, and poisons the sphere of the interhuman.

"Because genuine dialogue is an ontological sphere which is constituted by the authenticity of being, every invasion of semblance must damage it."[70] The very existence of the interhuman is threatened by a lie, and seeming to appear different from what one really is constitutes a lie. Man must exercise the ghost of semblance if he wants to free himself for the truth of being.

Speaking from his being, man communicates truth to the Other. This truth does not depend so much on what is being said as on how it is being said. The sphere of the interhuman need not be filled with effusive personal confessions or an exchange of confidences. Indiscrete overexposure is not truth. But dialogical partners must be frank with and must not hide their essential being from each Other. Just as primeval man was characterized as man by his upright walk, so dialogical man, Buber demands, ought to be characterized by the uprightness of his soul as he steers his course through the world of difficult social interrelationships into the realm of the interhuman.

There is, however, a special kind of seeming which Buber defines as "genuine seeming" When a youth is so affected by the personality of a man he encounters that he wants to emulate him as his hero, he is "seized by the actuality of heroism." There is nothing false in this particular situation which makes even an imitation into "genuine imitation."[71]

70 *Ibid.*, p. 112.

71 *Ibid.*, p. 112.

The interhuman in which man experiences his "stillest enthusiasms" is not circumscribed by a scientific horizon. It is permeated with the spirit of intuition which Buber prefers to call "imagining the real." Intuition, he explains, means looking at an Other (*Anschauung*). But imagining the real means "a bold swinging ... into the life of the Other"[72] which stirs man's being to its depth. Imagining the real brings fulfillment to the dialogue between man and man and makes it memorable beyond any other human experience.

> At such times, at each such time, the word arises in a substantial way between men who have been seized in their depths and opened out by the dynamic of an elemental togetherness. The interhuman opens out what otherwise remains unopened.[73]

---

72 *Ibid.*, p. 110.

73 *Ibid.*, pp. 112–113.

# Chapter 3

## ENCOUNTER: THE EMBODIMENT AND REALIZATION

### 1. Encounter: Its Embodiment and Realization in Marriage

As has been shown before,[1] "dialogic is not to be identified with love."[2] However, there can be no love without dialogic, that is, "without real outgoing to the Other."[3] Love is a "bipolar experience" in which I and Thou, basically different from and set over against each other, reach out to the beloved whom they draw close by "the strong-winged Eros of dialogue."[4] Both bipolarity of love and Eros of dialogue find their richest fulfillment and most meaningful expression in marriage.

Through dialogue as Eros, carried on in marriage, lover and beloved perceive, in enchanting simultaneousness, each other's sentiments and emotions which are part of the independent reality of husband and wife. The marital partners experience in their love the very essence of their own selfhood, while their most hidden I encounters its most hidden Thou. In the sensed unfolding of the Other, in utter mutual trust, lover and beloved share their moment of truth. Losing themselves, they find each other, and finding each other, they become more truly themselves in mutual realization and fulfillment.

Marriage is, for Buber, the encounter par excellence, exemplifying the relational nature of all being. And as encounter is also epistemologically significant,[5] marriage becomes a vehicle for attaining knowledge. For man cannot grasp the meaning of life by his rational power alone. He can know and understand only by relating himself to and involving

1 See p. 15, *Supra*.

2 Buber, "Dialogue," *Between Man and Man*, p. 21.

3 *Ibid*.

4 *Ibid*., p. 29.

5 See p. 15, *Supra*.

himself with an Other. The experience of sharing intimately the life of one Other being provides man with a deeper insight and a keener understanding of "was die Welt im Innersten zusammenhält"[6] than the widest possible experience he may have gathered among the endlessly varied phenomena of the world.

Life's secrets may defy solution of man's probing intellect. But through loving, and in love knowing and understanding an Other, man knows and understands the world. "The world is not comprehensible, but it is embraceable: through the embracing of one of its beings."[7] The beloved not only seems to fill or to represent the world, but he "indistinguishably coincides" with it in the experience of the lover.

All encounter, and especially marriage is marked by exclusiveness as well as by inclusiveness. It is exclusive in the sense of concerning only the partners themselves, but it is inclusive in the sense of potentially embracing the whole range of existence. Being absorbed in each other, I and Thou are ready to absorb the world, for their love makes them more sensitive to the needs as well as to the offerings of the world. In a genuine dialogue, the Thou means, implies, and "implicates the whole world"[8] for the I. Standing in the essential relation of "the community of marriage," man feels motivated to enter into an essential relation with the greater community of the world. For once the I has said "soul of my soul"[9] to its Thou, it has understood that life's richest gift lies in man's ability to relate himself to an Other.

A real (not a "fictitious") marriage with "its steady experiencing of the life-substance of the Other as the Other,"[10] with its crises and the overcoming of these crises, leads to insights indispensable to man's dealings with the body politic which is characterized by differences of background, faith, conviction, and concepts of truth and justice. As the "exemplary bond" tying the "two othernesses" of husband and wife together, marriage prepares man for life with the many othernesses he encounters in society, and for the recognition that mankind will

---

6 Johann Wolfgang von Goeth, *Faust*, Part I (Boston: DC Heath and Co., 1909), I, p. 22.

7 Buber, "With a Monist," *Pointing the Way*, p. 27.

8 Buber, *I and Thou*, p. 32.

9 *Ibid.*, p. 33.

10 Buber, "Question," *Between Man and Man*, p. 62.

eventually have to be united in the "greater bondage" of its positively affirmed interrelatedness.

As man and woman mutually experience their elemental otherness, they transcend their polarity and arrive at a fullness of being which neither could attain separately. Ideally, marriage achieves what Buber asks of any encounter: unification without obliteration of differences, and a heightened sense of wholeness based on the inclusion of the variegated and the distinct.

The individual is by nature ill equipped to face the world alone. He is, as it were, only half a human being. His incompleteness is somewhat reminiscent of the condition of the two halves into which Zeus split the originally unified man-woman creature, according to Aristophanes' description in Plato's *Symposium*.[11] As the two halves in Aristophanos' tale must forever yearn for reunification in and through love which would bring about a "healing of the state of man," so Buber's I must meet its Thou and in through this encounter restore man's primal state of "wesenhafte Zweifältigkeit."[12]

Marriage, more than any other elation, succeeds in reestablishing this primal state of unified duality by the mutual contribution of man and wife. Giving of their own being, they complete each Other's being. The shared intimacy of their life together is a constant dialogue whose very continuance enhances every moment of their existence.

True marriage is not built out of two I's, but by "the central Thou" which "is the metaphysical and metapsychical factor of love to which feelings of love are mere accompaniments."[13] A marriage is both an institution and a state of feelings, with the institution providing "the consent form," and the feelings "the changing content." But form and content, institution and feelings put together still do not result in the loving relation of the marital encounter. Only "the central presence of the Thou"[14] creates the dimension in which marriage can exist, and from which it derives its meaning.

11 Plato, "Symposium," *The Philosophy of Plato*, trans. Jewett, ed. Irwin Edman (New York: The Modern Library, 1956), pp. 353–358.

12 Martin Buber, *Ich und Du* (Leipzig: Inselverlag, 1913), p. 20.

13 Buber, *I and Thou*, p. 46.

14 *Ibid.*

This central Thou is for the marriage partners what the sphere of the Interhuman is for any individual encountering each other—the realm where they have their "real being." Marriage is the rootedness and the at-homeness of two I's in the centrality of the Thou. It is that "enrapturing dynamic of relation"[15] in which I and Thou most essentially live, a union that enlarges rather than dissolves their self-being.

Buber's views on marriage have stirring religious overtones. While he says that any encounter of I and Thou "happens" by an act of grace,[16] he is filled with a special sense of wonder at the "narrow ridge" of marital love. For this one fully reciprocal relation whose lasting actuality and certainty make it unique in a world of bewildering relational possibilities and uncertainties seems to come about not only by grace, nor by man's own power of volition, but by something akin to a miracle.

In its entwining of one life with another, marriage is the sacramental affirmation of an I that the Other *is*. Only by affirming and sharing in this being of the Other can man affirm and share in the "Present Being" of God. And only by being answerable for an Other who is entrusted to him can man answer "the lifelong address of God."[17] In this sense, "love is responsibility of an I for a Thou"[18]—not just a feeling or an emotion, but a state of total commitment to and tender care for an Other.

Buber contrasts his own view on marriage with that of Kierkegaard who broke his engagement to Regina Olsen because he was afraid that marriage would be an impediment to his exclusive dedication to God. Buber remonstrates with Kierkegaard that to renounce one's love for this reason "is sublimely to misunderstand God."[19] Rather than being a hurdle which keeps man from reaching God, love can serve as the very road to Him. For

> we are created along with one another and directed to a life with one another. Creatures are placed in my way so that I, their

15 *Ibid.*, p. 87.

16 See p. 17, *Supra.*

17 Buber, "Question," *Between Man and Man*, p. 61.

18 Buber, *I and Thou*, p. 15.

19 Buber, "Question," *Between Man and Man*, p. 52.

> fellow creature, by means of them and with them find the way to God. … God wants us to come to him by means of the Reginas he has created and not by renunciation of them.[20]

It is inconceivable that God, the creator of all life, should regard marriage as detrimental to man's glorification of His name. For marriage, as Buber wants it understood, is the ultimate sanctification of life, perpetuating it not only physically, but creating it, as it were, ever anew metaphysically, by calling into being an I and a Thou.

Buber feels that "a God in whom only the parallel lines of single approaches intersect is more akin to the 'God of the philosophers' than to the 'God of Abraham and Isaac and Jacob.'"[21] That is, Kierkegaard's God, the God of the lonely individual, of the "Single One," seems to Buber life-less, a construct of the intellect only. He himself conceives of God as "the God of all lives in whom all life is fulfilled."[22] It would not be in keeping with the nature of this "living God" to exclude any of His creatures from His presence, or to demand that they renounce their closest possible and most life-giving relationship.

In Buber's view, marriage does not block man's view of the Holy but, quite to the contrary, it affords him a glimpse of eternity. For though impermanence is inherent in the human condition, the sustained I-Thou relation of husband and wife with its unquestioning reliance on the being-there of the Other strengthens, by implication, man's reliance on the permanent being-there of God. The certainty of and trust in a human Thou leads man to certainty of and trust in a Divine Thou, "the Thou in which the parallel lines of relation meet."[23]

## 2. Encounter: Its Embodiment and Realization in Religion

Any Thou man pronounces expresses an essential relation between himself and an Other. There is no "unessential and fundamentally invalid" Thou, for all genuine encounter between man and man is

---

20 *Ibid.*

21 *Ibid.*

22 *Ibid.*

23 Buber, *I and Thou*, p. 33.

meaningful. But in addition to having a value all its own, it transcends its necessarily limited realm and points beyond itself, towards a greater meaning and an absolute value. "In being together the unlimited and the unconditioned is experienced" because "human life touches on absoluteness in virtue of its dialogical character."[24]

Every human Thou, though called into existence through the address of a human I, has its real being in God. For no matter how enduring a relationship between man and man may be, it is in the nature of things that a human Thou must be temporary. But God is man's "eternal Thou" which "by its nature cannot become It."[25] Between God and man there exists a permanent dialogical relation in which God speaks to man through all of His creation, and man addresses the everlastingly Present One as his Thou.

Buber rejects the theory that God is an idea, or a non-projected image of highest perfection. Nor must God be considered as immanent in the world or in the human self, though he comprises both universe and man. He defines God as a living reality, existing absolutely independently of man, yet willing to enter into a mutual relation with him.

God cannot be defined as either personal or impersonal. He must be understood to be "both the boundless and nameless as well as the father who teaches His children to address Him."[26] God's impersonal, "pure" divinity is unaddressable, says Buber, but this divinity is augmented by God as person, as an I who addresses man as Thou ("Thou shalt"), and whom man, in turn, can address as his Thou. God's personality can also be understood to be His act. But whatever the definition—God is the Absolute, and in His absoluteness He is the eminently Other, but an Other which man can encounter and apprehend.

Man apprehends God neither through his intellect alone nor through his feelings and emotions only. Rather, he apprehends God by relating himself to Him with all he is and all he has—body, soul, and spirit together becoming an instrument for the reception of the Divine

---

24 Buber, "What is Man?" *Between Man and Man*, p. 168.

25 Buber, *I and Thou*, p. 75.

26 Martin Buber, *The Origin and Meaning of Ḥasidism*, ed. and trans. M. Friedman (New York: Horizon Press, 1960), pp. 92–93.

message, and for understanding and answering its personal address. God, dialogically experienced, is a voice men can hear, but never a form or shape he can see. But having no recognizable "Gestalt" is not equivalent with being amorphous. God is a very definitely and concretely felt presence, a force which sustains a continuity of "relational events." In and through these relational events, that is encounters, God communicates His will to man who can thus recognize Him as a Thou.

Buber feels that an I-Thou encounter with God is so intensely personal as to elude the restrictions organized religion tries to impose upon it. The fluidity of the living relation between God and man turns stagnant when forced into the rigid forms of an established ritual. The God of institutionalized convention is not the "Lord of existence" whose voice man hears in the polyphony of life. Organized religion in is the chrysalis form of "The Word" spoken by that voice—and only a personal encounter between God and man can transform it from its earthbound stage—and give it new wings.

When religion becomes a system, it may offer man a sense of orientation by providing him with a set of rules which regulate his life. But it is also liable to lose its spirit of immediacy, and therefore its power of inspiration. The arch of the temple-dome, says Buber, can easily obstruct man's view of the firmament.

An institutionalized approach to God forecloses all possibility of encountering Him face to face. All too often, religious observance becomes a matter of mere calendar-observance of a string of feast- and fast-days. But calendar-observance has very little to do with true religiosity. The truly religious person does not even need a set time or any particular place for praying. "Ordered devotional exercises"[27] are neither prayers nor I-Thou encounters. Man, longing for some tangible extension into space of his "pure" relation to God, tends to make God the object of a cult. But an objectified God is an inauthentic God, for He is seen as an It rather than addressed by "the holy primary word" Thou. The immediacy of God's presence, experienced in an I-Thou encounter is replaced by the media of cult and rite. But the only assurance man has

27 Buber, *I and Thou*, p. 114.

of God's continued presence lies in encountering this presence over anew in a direct I-Thou relation.

Buber sees the members of a religious organization as a community of "organized believers" who form a circle around a center. Man's relations to their Eternal Thou ought to be like radial lines running from this circle to the center. But the organized believer often mistakes the periphery of the circle for its focal point. Failing to be a radius connecting the rim of the communal wheel with its hub, he fails to be aware of the radiance and warmth emanating from this hub.

The religious life of the organized believer is so governed by rules and regulations that the meticulous observance of ritual forms often assumes a greater importance for him than an understanding of the content these forms were meant to guard. Buber does not deny the necessity of laws and commandments. But he feels they are meaningful only as long as they really "mean" the persona whom they address. The grandeur and lasting validity of the Ten Commandments stem from the fact that they address man as a personal Thou rather than as a collective you. Though the Decalogue was given to an entire people and, implicitly, to all the generations to come, each individual who ever listened to it must understand that it was given to him personally, and that "the Thou in it is no one else but one's own self."[28]

But when what was intended to be an unconditionally personal command becomes a very conditional impersonal maxim, its particular hold on the individual is loosened. Universally accepted and objectified into neutrality, "maxims command only the third person, the each and the none."[29] The question arises, though, whether it is not just its strong personal appeal that turns a command into a maxim. Universal acceptance of a law need not necessarily rob it of its original meaning, but may, on the contrary, contribute to its translation into reality. A universally accepted maxim would, then, not vaguely command the each and the none, but very definitely the one and the all.

28 Buber, "Education of Character," *Between Man and Man*, p. 114.

29 *Ibid.*

Buber reverently affirms the dialogical spirit of "... the 'I' of the speaking God and the 'thou' of the hearing Israel."[30] He hears in the Bible quite literally the voice of God pronouncing His moral law which is absolutely binding. But he denies the ritual law its claim upon man's unquestioning obedience. Man must have the right to accept what he considers to be of significance to him, and to reject what seems to him without value. Man must be permitted to distinguish in his innermost being between what is and what is not commanded him personally. If religion is to be a dialogue between God and man, its laws and commandments must "say something" to the individual to whom they are directed, and whom they want to direct.

Buber's insistence on man's right to decide for himself in matters of religious observance has exposed him to the charge of "religious anarchism."[31] But he neither recommends religious lawlessness in general, nor even the rash overthrowing of any particular law. He merely suggests that man should not be forced by an authority or convention to keep a law which has become so ossified under the accumulated layers of outworn traditions that all life seems to have been choked out of it.

Buber warns repeatedly of the danger of developing a false sense of security by over-reliance on the judgment of others. In religious as well as in all other matters, man must do his own thinking. Taking upon himself the burden of freedom of conscience, he must search for his own "uncertain certainty." Conscientiously examining the issue under consideration, he will try to penetrate the shell of the It which convention has formed around the heart of the matter, its Thou. Only after such an examination will he be able to decide responsibly on what should be kept, and what discarded. "With my choice and action—committing or omitting, acting or preserving—I answer the word, however inadequately, yet properly; I answer for my hour."[32]

---

30 Martin Buber, *The Prophetic Faith*, trans. Carlyle Witton Davies (New York: Macmillan Co., 1949), p. 54.

31 Gershom Scholem, "Martin Bubers Deutung des Chassidissus," *Literatur und Kunst, Neue Zürcher Zeitung*, (Fernausgabe No. 142, May 1962).

32 Buber, "Question," *Between Man and Man*, p. 68.

Making his free choice, man does not only answer for his own hours. As each man's hour and its task are inseparably interrelated with an Other's, his decisions and actions affect not only the Other but also determine, to a degree, the shape of the future.

Buber's deep awareness of the far-reaching consequences of man's actions provides the needed counter-balance to his highly subjective attitude towards authority. He advocates a constant check of this subjectivity and the subsequent relativity of values by a severely uncompromising confrontation of the human I with the absoluteness of the Eternal Thou. His encounter with God is man's ultimate criterion of truth; therefore, before he will decide on the relevance of a handed-down tradition, this tradition "... must be reforged in the fire of the truth of his personal essential relation to the Absolute if it is to win true validity."[33]

Religion, not shored up by institutional scaffolding, is a "risk." Full of the spirit of daring, it is a venture of the heart and mind to conquer their own frontiers. A genuinely religious person is not impervious to error, for he may either fail to hear, or else he may misinterpret God's address. But he can be certain that through his total commitment to God, that is through living from his being towards God's being, his "mortal bit of life"[34] partakes of eternity.

Unsupported by religious dogmata which assure the organized believer of his spiritual safety, the religiously independent thinker lives in the "holy insecurity" of walking the narrow ridge.[35] He is fully conscious of the precariousness of his position, yet he is firmly convinced that there is no Other, and certainly never a safely prescribed way for him to meet God.

> O you secure and safe ones who hide yourselves behind the defense-works of the law so that you will not have to look into God's abyss! Yes, you have secure ground under your feet while we hang suspended, looking out over the endless deeps. But we would not exchange our dizzy insecurity and our poverty for your security and abundance. For to you God is one who created

33 Buber, "Religion and Ethics," *Eclipse of God*, p. 98.

34 Buber, "Dialogue," *Between Man and Man*, p. 14.

35 See p. 28, *Supra*.

> once and not again; but to us God is He who "renews the work of creation every day.' To you God is one who revealed himself once and no more; but to us He speaks out of the burning thou-bush of the present ... in the revelations of our innermost heart ... greater than words.[36]

In spite of his severe objections to many of the traditional aspects of religion in general and Judaism in particular, Buber's credo that all life is encounter is rooted in Judaism, or at least in his concept of Judaism. He feels deeply that as a Jew he is part of a people whose entire history is based on the "relational event" of revelation, and whose historical *raison d'être* is to keep the spirit of this event, "the dialogue between heaven and earth," alive.

Therefore, the Jew must not permit his past to become a thing of the past. He must integrate it into his every-day life which he hallows by being a witness to God's living presence. This presence is evident not only throughout history, but every man is confronted with it in the here and now—in his here and now.

Man has a tendency to evade personal confrontations—with men, with ideas, with issues. It is safer to think of so overwhelming a happening as a Divine revelation in terms of the past than as a possibility of the present, and it is easier to accept it as having happened to someone else than to consider the staggering possibility of its happening to oneself. "Revelation will tolerate no perfect tense, but man with the arts of his craze for security props it up into perfectedness."[37]

Just as God's act of revelation must not be relegated to the past, so Buber does not want His act of creation narrowly understood as a one-time event, done and finished by Divine fiat. Creation is a present-tense, every ongoing dialogue between God and man. Buber shares Judaism's view that man is God's partner who can and must participate in perfecting and eventually redeeming the world. Man can collaborate with God in creating the world by re-creating himself as an ever more human human-being.

---

36 Martin Buber, "Der Heilige Weg," *Reden über das Judentum*, 1919, pp. 65, 71; trans. and quoted M.S. Friedman, *Martin Buber, The Life of Dialogue*, p. 262.

37 Buber, "Dialogue," *Between Man and Man*, p. 18.

God called the world and man into being. It is now up to man who answered God's call once by coming into existence, to answer Him again by giving direction and meaning to this existence. A meaningful existence is directed towards other existences—God's and men's. It is an existence of the loving deed, of social action, and of constructive use of man's natural endowments. Man, in short, answers God's act of creation with his set of being—that is, of entering into relation to others:

> God in all concreteness as speaker, the creation as speech: God's call into nothing and the answer of things through their coming into existence, the speech of creation enduring in the life of all creation, the life of each creature as dialogue, the world as word—to proclaim this Israel existed. It taught, it showed that the real God is the God who can be addressed because he is the God who addresses.[38]

Man accepts what God has created, says Buber, not in order to possess it, but in order to complete the incomplete. "God wills to need man for the work of completing His creation."[39] For creation is "an ever-recurrent happening" in which man participates by his own creative work. One of the most glaring imperfections of the world is the discord between man and man, so that it is man's most pressing task to achieve world harmony. In support of this view Buber cites the old Jewish saying that the man who works for peace is the companion of God in the work of creation.

A life of creation can never be a life of seclusion. Creative man does not live in an esoterically spiritual atmosphere high above the earthly and occasionally earthy concerns of the lowly and the downtrodden. He tackles life's problems where he finds them, for only by working from out of their midst can he create conditions that will help to eliminate them. "Our mission is not to the realms in which dwells the purity of holiness; it is to the unholy that we must pay attention so that it find redemption and become whole."[40]

---

38 *Ibid.*, pp. 91–92.

39 Buber, *Origin and Meaning of Ḥasidism*, p. 104.

40 Martin Buber, *For the Sake of Heaven*, trans. L. Lewisohn (Philadelphia: The Jewish Publication Society of America, 1945), p. 117.

The Jewish prayer which praises God. For renewing His work of creation every day impresses Buber deeply. He is convinced that God "waits" for man to help Him with this renewal by which the world will be carried forward towards the fullness of time. But this carrying forward must not be understood as an evolutionary or as a historical process through which a better world will eventually emerge. It ought to be understood as man's sustained attempt to re-create the "relational event" of the original creation by casting his every-day in its mould, that is by making the world his Thou.

The fullness of time will then not be projected into eternity as "a mystical timeless now," but it will announce itself "as a bodily happening in the world, out of the concrete meeting between God and men."[41] The fullness of time is the fullness of life lived in relation to God and to man. Man becomes God's partner in redeeming the world by his "redemption of the everyday," that is, by taking on and trying to discharge to the best of his ability the task of the hour.

Convinced of the fundamental importance of dialogic as man's basic attitude not only towards his fellow-man, but also towards God, Buber does not think that theology can contribute anything really essential to man's relation with God For theology speaks *about* God in the abstract terms of It, while man must speak *to* God in the concrete terms of an I-Thou encounter. "I-Thou finds its highest intensity and transfiguration in religious reality, in which unlimited Being becomes, as absolute person, my partner."[42]

The God of theology (like the God of the philosophers) is a theoretical abstract rather than a living reality. This abstract is set in an "above," unreachable, incommunicado, forever apart from man's "below," and from his need for a life of communication. But for Buber, lastingly influenced by Ḥasidism,[43] there must be no separate realms of the theoretical and the practical, the holy and the profane, the religious and the secular. Life refuses to be compartmentalized. Neither ethics nor morals nor religion must be stowed away and saved, as it were, for special occasions when their use seems to be warranted. If religion, as it

41 Buber, *Origin and Meaning of Ḥasidism*, pp. 106–107.

42 Buber, "Religion and Philosophy," *Eclipse of God*, pp. 44–45.

43 See p. 3, *Supra*.

occasionally does, accepts the suggestion of theology that "religious" things are more worthy of man's concern that "secular" ones, it is no longer really integrated in his life, but has become a sham instead. "Meeting with God does not come to man in order that he may concern himself with God, but in order that he may confirm that there is meaning in the world."[44]

When Buber warns against relegating religion to the realm of the extra-ordinary, he is not only thinking of its institutionalized form. He is just as concerned with the unconventionally pious individual who, in his thirst for knowing God, longs for a mystic union with Him. Buber understands such a man's motivations only too well, for he, too, sought and occasionally attained states of religious ecstasy in his youth.

But he has come to feel that what man considers a mystic union with God is only a mystic union with himself. Rather than ascending to God, ecstatic man descends into the deepest recesses of his own soul. Man cannot fuse his being with God's. God must remain the ever Other whom man can meet, but with whom he cannot become one. Even during the unparalleled closeness of their encounter, the distinction between man and God cannot be obliterated. Man remains man, an I. God remains God, a Thou; and the human I cannot lose itself in the Eternal Thou, but must keep its separate identity. Man's soul is and remains his alone, "existing but once, single, unique, irreducible, this creaturely one: one of the human souls and not the 'soul of the All'; a defined and particular being and not "Being'."[45]

Man cannot become one with God in wordless union, but he can confront the Absolute in the dynamic relation of a dialogical encounter which gives spiritual meaning to his entire life rather than to some "'deified' exalted hours."[46] These rare hours are not representative of religious experience. Man encounters God both "in his despairs and in his raptures."[47] But "the religious" must not be equated with "the exceptional," to be experienced only in moments of elation which seem

44 Buber, *I and Thou,* p. 115.

45 Buber, "Dialogue," *Between Man and Man,* p. 24.

46 *Ibid.,* p. 25.

47 Buber, "Religion and Reality," *Eclipse of God,* p. 20.

to carry man into come beyond. To be truly enthralled with God is to be truly enthralled with life.

Recognizing that God speaks to him through the world, man also recognizes that "God, indeed, is not the cosmos, but far less is he Being *minus* cosmos."[48] To serve God therefore means to accept as justified, and to respond to "each mortal hour's fullness of claim and responsibility."[49] If that attitude can be called religion, says Buber, then religion "is just *everything*, simply all that is lived in its possibility of dialogue."[50] And the possibility of dialogue is as large as life itself.

Actualizing life's dialogical potential, man lives ethically, trying "to help God by loving his creation in his creatures, by loving it towards Him."[51] Loving God's creation, man anticipates and attempts to meet the needs of others. Hearing the call from "above" in the voice of every creature in the "below" of their shared world, he interconnects "above" and "below" by living dialogically. For speaking to man, he speaks, by implication, to God, and speaking to God, he speaks to man. Relating himself to God, man dedicates his entire being to Him.

Buber insists in all his writings that immediacy is indispensable in any I-Thou encounter. In fact, his derogatory treatment of organized religion stems largely from his conviction that it prevents man from encountering God in immediacy. Yet he reiterates again and again not only that man's love of God begins with his love of man, but that God is best encountered through encountering the world: "Meet the world with the fullness of your being and you shall meet Him. That He Himself accepts from your hands what you have to give to the world, is His mercy. If you wish to believe, love!"[52] And when he says that "real relationship to God cannot be achieved on earth if real relationships to the world and to mankind are lacking,"[53] one might assume that he considers man-with-man as mediator for the man-God encounter.

However, he goes on to say that "both love of the Creator and love of that which He has created are finally one and the same." If loving one's

48 Buber, "Question," *Between Man and Man*, p. 58.

49 Buber, "Dialogue," *Between Man and Man*, p. 14.

50 *Ibid.*

51 Buber, "Question," *Between Man and Man*, p. 57.

52 Buber, *At the Turning* p. 44.

53 *Ibid.*

fellow-man and the world is but another way of loving God, then man's relation to man does not mediate his relation to God. In Buber's view, a human Thou does not stand between man and God, nor does the world. Rather, God and man are connected by a line of communication which runs straight through man's Thou and through the world he encounters. Both man's Thou and the world act as transmitters for the dialogical word between God and man. But man also brings his human Thou and his world to God by dedicating his relations with them to the Eternal Thou in whom, Buber says, all relations are consummated.

It is Buber's contention that man need not ever seek God, for there is no area or event in life empty of God.[54] Man therefore finds God simply by living, and by making His presence "real" to himself as he consciously sees all things in God, and God in all things. God's presence is "self-evident," and he is nearer to man than man is to himself. Yet He is not to be found by introspection. Man cannot find Him by carrying on a conversation with his own soul. He is found, or rather His reality is recognized, only in a direct dialogical relation. This relation cannot be established exclusively in either the physical or the metaphysical realm of man's life. It is all-inclusive: "Men do not find God if they stay in the world. They do not find Him if they leave the world. He who goes out with his whole being to meet His Thou and carries to it all being that is in the world, finds Him who cannot be sought."[55]

In accordance with Judaism's central teaching that God is One, Buber expresses his personal belief in the absolute unity of God. But he introduces the metaphysical concept of "moment God"[56] to describe the way in which alone man can apprehend God's Oneness. God speaks to us, as was shown before, through the various relations we have with men and things. That is, we apprehend Him, the One and Eternal God, through all our momentary meetings with "the God of a moment." We understand God's unified wholeness behind the seeming fragmentation of His world much in the way in which we comprehend the personality

54 See the motto on the flyleaf of *I and Thou*: "So, waiting, I have won from you the end: God's presence in each element" (Goethe).

55 Buber, *I and Thou*, p. 79.

56 Buber, "Dialogue," *Between Man and Man*, p. 15.

of a poet and the meaning of his message by reading all of his works, not just selected pieces.

The realization that behind the many there is the One constitutes our faith, and it also compels us not to shun the many, but to recognize them for what they are, or what they potentially can be: God's very abode to which we, too, will be admitted—if we are willing to pay the price of human involvement in the manifoldness of life: "... 'faith' is not a feeling in the soul of man but an entrance into reality."[57]

In Buber's hierarchy of values, man's highest good lies in establishing essential relations. Conversely, the individual's failure to establish meaningful relationships results in evil.[58] When man chooses self-centered rather than relational living, and when he ruthlessly pursues his own ends without regard for others, he becomes a sinner.

Buber, in accordance with Jewish tradition, does not believe in original sin. Man, he says, "sins as Adam sinned, and not because Adam sinned."[59] One must, however, make a distinction between the sinner and the wicked. The sinner misses the mark set for him by God. Because proneness to error is inherent in man's condition, he will trespass over the demarcation line between good and evil and become an evil-doer. But equally inherent in man is his freedom of choice and of action. Therefore, realizing that he has gone astray, the sinner can decide to turn around, and to make a new and better start. His turning is a re-turning, full of hope for redemption, for he knows that God forgives those who turn to Him.

But the wicked is evil by disposition. He does not miss the mark—he fails to try for it. Never having turned to God, he cannot re-turn. He sins

---

57 Buber, "Prelude, Report on Two Talks," *Eclipse of God*, p. 3.

58 Expressed in a somewhat different terminology, this view on evil might be compared with the view of Plotinus on the same subject: "If evil exist at all, it must be situated in the realm of non-being. By this non-being we are not to understand something that simply does not exist, but only something of an utterly different order from Authentic Being. ..." *The Essence of Plotinus*, compiled by Grace H. Trumbull, based on Mackenna translation (New York: Oxford University Press, 1948), p. 55. In Buber's philosophy, being is being-with, that is relation. Lack of relation is therefore inauthentic being, or non-being. Since lack of relation is evil, non-being is evil.

59 Martin Buber, *Two Types of Faith*, trans. N.P. Goldhaws (New York: Harper Torchbooks, Harper and Brothers, 1951), p. 158.

not because he has lost his way—his sin is that he was not ever on his way. He never even searches for a way to God, for he does not recognize his creatureliness and the subsequent necessity of the primal movement, the turning-towards.[60] He therefore cuts himself off irredeemably from the creator whom he denies.

The man who is aware of his creatureliness, however, affirms his belief in a personal God by the act of turning. An impersonal God cannot be encountered as Thou. One cannot pray to an idea, nor can one face a power that operates in silent aloofness, unrelated to the life of the individual. But when an I, in need of linking its personal existence with an absolute existence which it dimly perceives, decodes on turning towards this Absolute, it turns "... not towards the remoteness, but towards a nearness and intimacy ..."[61] of a Thou whose presence makes itself unmistakably and almost physically felt.

Buber feels that the process of turning to God (Hebrew: *teshuvah*) is misleadingly called repentance. It ought to be understood in its original literal meaning as "something which happens in the immediacy of the reality in which men and God are together."[62] Turning, he is convinced, is not just a psychic phenomenon. It is a total seizure of the entire person.

> Turning is as little an event falling within the soul of man as man's birth or death; it comes upon the whole person, it is carried by the whole person, and does not take place in the intercourse of a man with himself but in the simple reality of the ur-reciprocity.[63]

This statement is not quite clear. It would appear that turning is a voluntary act, based on and following man's free decision to change the inner direction of his life. But if it is a voluntary act, it cannot possibly be compared to birth or death which, as natural processes, are outside of man's power of volition. Turning as such may indeed be more than merely a psychological phenomenon; it may be man's answer to an existentially felt need. But the decision preceding the act of turning

---

60 See pp. 33–35, *Supra*.

61 Buber, *Two Types of Faith*, p. 157.

62 Buber, "Faith of Judaism," *Mamre*, p. 8.

63 *Ibid*.

must doubtlessly be the result of considerations "falling within the soul of man."

Moreover, Buber seems to regard what he calls "ur-reciprocity" as a given datum of life. As such, it would, however, be part of a predetermined situation. It would lack the spontaneity without which, by definition, encounter cannot come about. Buber's emphasis, throughout his work, on man's placement in a concrete existential situation, and his equally strong insistence upon man's freedom of choice and of action result, at times, in a strange contradiction.

When Buber says that the relation between God and man is characterized by reciprocity, he speaks with the assurance of one who believes in the everlasting willingness of God to be man's Eternal Thou, a dialogical partner who speaks and who listens. God's voice is always audible—if only man would not put wax into his ears to shut out the sound. There are, admittedly, occasions when man, far from turning a deaf ear to God, still either does not hear His voice at all, or else feels utterly rejected by what he hears. But even then he does not have sufficient reason to doubt that God reciprocates his turning to Him. Quite to the contrary, there is every reason for man to hold fast to his faith, for only then can he hope to have God's will revealed to him.

For though God's presence is self-evident,[64] His reciprocity is not. It is, as it were, latently there—but it is man's responsibility to make it evident to himself:

> The whole meaning of reciprocity, indeed, lies in just this, that it does not wish to impose itself but to be freely apprehended. It gives us something to apprehend, but it does not give us the apprehension. Our act must be entirely our own for that which is to be disclosed to us to be disclosed, even that which must disclose each individual to himself.[65]

However, Buber realizes that it is one of the most perplexing religious problems to "apprehend freely" the meaning, or even only the existence, of a reciprocal relationship between God and man. The

64 See p. 27, *Supra.*

65 Buber, "Religion and Ethics," *Eclipse of God*, pp. 98–99.

problem is thrown into relief in all its complexity in his discussion of suffering.

All encounter, including man's encounter with God, is characterized by action. That is, the I must perform the act of turning towards the Thou, and must go forward to meet it. But if it happens that in spite of his eager action no Divine encounter is granted to man, yet if he still persists in his hope for one, his relation to God will be marked by enforced passivity and by suffering.

The "suffering servant" of Deutero-Isaiah, to whom Buber refers in his discussion of the problem of reciprocity between God and man, prepares for meeting God by patient waiting. He is no more than an arrow, kept concealed in the quiver of God. But he keeps himself in readiness, in glad anticipation of a time when God will decide to take him out of his dark, confining concealment, and to put him to use.

Here encounter is not the dramatic face-to-face meeting between God and man which gives religious purpose and vitality to man's life. It is rather an undramatic and often tragic and frustrating state of enduring, an uncomplaining wait for God's attention. The suffering servant, though as yet unrecognized and unnoticed, does not give up the hope to be sought out by God in His own good time, and to be activated as an instrument in carrying out His will. His very suffering is his action—his act of faith.

Buber asserts that God's voice can always be heard in and through nature, for nature gives clear evidence of His uninterrupted act of creation. This is what the psalmist means when he says that the heavens and the earth "declare" the glory of God. But in history, God's voice is heard only in the peak hours of revelation. These "times of great utterance," in which man can recognize the Divine power behind events, alternate with "mute times" which seem to be devoid of God's presence, so that man finds it difficult to uphold his faith in God as his dialogical partner. Isaiah (8:17) speaks already of a time when God "hideth His face from the house of Jacob," and when the events of some particularly dark hours of history seem so "barbarous" that man finds it impossible to consider them Divine deeds.

It is exceedingly hard to accept and to understand a concept of God who alternately reveals and conceals[66] Himself. The suffering servant, however, simply bears his affliction of being cut off from God's presence, sustained by his firm belief that this will only be a momentary separation and not a final severance. If God's face seems to be hidden from him, he will resign himself to a period of encounter-less darkness whose reason he does not question.

For as man can be certain of the sun's reappearance even after a total eclipse, so the suffering servant holds on to his certainty of God's eventual reappearance in his personal life and in the world, in spite of what might appear to be God-forsaken periods. "That He hides Himself does not diminish the immediacy: in the immediacy He remains the Saviour."[67] As Job did not feel abandoned by God in spite of his sore afflictions, so the suffering servant, be he an individual or a historical group, will not submit to a feeling of having been deserted. Encounter between God and man is not only a continuous personal and historical possibility, but it is an ever-present reality. In his dialogue with God, man must be ready to respond even before he is called, for he can be certain that eventually the call will come.

But, asks Buber, taking up a question put to him after the European Holocaust, how is a life with God still possible in a time when millions have been killed in extermination camps, when

> "… the estrangement has become too cruel, the hiddenness too deep. … Can one still, as an individual or as a people, enter at all into a dialogic relationship with Him? Can one still call to Him? Dare we recommend to the survivors of Oswiecim [Auschwitz], the Job of the gas changers: 'Call to Him, for He is kind, for His mercy endureth forever'"?[68]

Buber does not minimize the agony of man who wants to believe, yet whose belief seems to be turned into cruel mockery by the soul-shaking atrocity of a man-made catastrophe whose dimensions stagger the mind. The abominations which have happened cannot be made undone. Today as in Job's day, God offers neither explanation of justification for

66 Isaiah 45:15.

67 Buber, *Two Types of Faith*, p. 169.

68 Buber, "The Dialogue between Heaven and Earth," *At the Turning*, p. 61.

the evil which he permitted to rage unchecked. The Biblical cry, "the judge of all the earth, will He not do justice?!" seems to go unheeded once again. And still, Buber clings to his credo of a living God who can be encountered as man's Eternal Thou. For though God as Thou may, for unfathomable reasons, go into hiding, He has not ceased to exist. Even the hidden is there—though its presence may not be evident. God does answer man's call—but not by setting right the wrong, nor by transferring cruelty into kindness, nor by making adjustments as the manager of a complaint department might do.

God's true answer is to be found in what Buber considers His "appearance," that is, His resumption of a temporarily disrupted dialogue. He points to Job, the symbol of unexplained and probably unexplainable suffering, who, having endured God's terrifying distance, was finally able to feel His nearness again. The disaster that had befallen him could not be nullified; yet Job could see, hear, and "know" God again in His new appearance.

Buber refuses to admit the possibility that God might end His dialogue with man; but again he shifts the responsibility for its continuance to man.[69] The Eternal Thou will never become a non-caring It. If man will only persist in his role as partner of God by continuing his tenacious struggle against human evil, and if he will keep alive his faculty of human responsiveness, he will become aware once again of God's partnership. He will once more hear God's voice, and understand what it says. Sometime, somehow the dreadful eclipse of God will be over, and man will again recognize His face, no longer hidden, but shining upon him in the closeness of their encounter.

What Buber says here is doubtlessly of therapeutic value to the survivors of a particular historical or of a personal tragedy. It shines a ray of hope to those whose suffering has thrown them into an abyss of doubt and despair. But it fails to explain, as does the Book of Job itself, the suffering of those who did not survive. Why did Job's sons and daughters have to die? Why were six million human beings permitted to be hounded, tortured, exterminated? Why did their Eternal Thou go into hiding just when they needed it most? Why did their terror-stricken outcry meet stony silence?

---

69 See p. 84, *Supra*.

An eclipse is recognized as a passing stage only by those who see its end. For them, there is an answer, because there is a new beginning: the sun has re-appeared. But for those who die during or because of the darkness, there is no answer. Their night does not pass. They pass into the night. They may have frantically searched for the faintest glimmer of the Hidden Face—but there is no knowing whether they ever saw it.

It seems that Buber, by using the metaphor of the eclipse of God, has done no more than give a description of the conditions during which man suffers what appears to be an unjust and undeserved fate. But a description can neither explain nor justify a happening which defies every attempt at understanding.

Buber is, of course, quite aware that "for one who believes in the living God, who knows about Him and is fated to spend his life in a time of His hiddenness, it is very difficult to live."[70] He realizes that in spite of his trying to find a way out of the terrible dilemma of the doubting believer, "the mystery has remained unsolved."[71] Man can, he therefore finally concludes, do no more than accept "the inscrutableness" of the "unknowable" and, in acceptance and in pain, still believe in God, revealed, or concealed, and love Him.

Believing in God and loving Him, he will believe in the world and love it, affirming its pain along with its joy.

> The believing man who goes through the gate of dread is directed to the concrete contextual situations of his existence ... he endures in the face of God the reality of livid life, dreadful and incomprehensible though it be. He loves it in the love of God, when he has learned to love.[72]

But though man must accept the concrete situation as it is given to him, he need not "accept that which meets him as 'God-given' in its pure factuality."[73] He will indeed enter into any concrete, given situation, but he may at times find it necessary to fight that situation and the conditions which brought it about. For he may consider its very

70 Buber, "The Dialogue between Heaven and Earth," *At the Turning,* p. 60.

71 *Ibid..,* p. 62.

72 Buber, "Religion and Philosophy," *Eclipse of God,* pp. 37.

73 *Ibid.*

"givenness" a challenge to his intellectual powers which are equally "given" to him.

Acceptance of the inscrutable will of God and acceptance of a given status quo are two entirely different things. God's will is and must remain an absolute mystery. But any status quo is a "relative mystery" which might conceivably yield its secret to the scrutiny of the human mind, and which might be solved by man's tireless efforts. Piety is not passivity. Nor is spirituality divorced from reality. A truly religious person knows his creaturely limitations. But within these limitations, he does his utmost to become a creator, and to be a co-worker of God, so that the interrupted dialogue between heaven and earth will be resumed again in the reality of life.

Seen in this way, it seems possible to speak of an ever-ongoing dialogue between God and man, though it is invariably the human partner who is charged with its continuance in a tangible form.

Discussing the reciprocity of the I-Thou relation between man and nature,[74] it was suggested that man who approaches a tree in the Thou-attitude becomes the tree's guarantor, vouchsafing its being, and that the fact that man recognizes the tree's "presence" constitutes the reciprocity of their I-Thou relation.

By analogy, it might now be suggested that man's living dialogically as a "witness" vouchsafes God's dialogical presence as man's eternal Thou. But it remains questionable whether Buber is justified to speak of reciprocity at all in a relationship between two entities that must forever remain different from one another, not as a matter of degree, but as a matter of principle. If God is, by definition, the absolutely Other and therefore utterly beyond compare, how can it be said of Him that He reciprocates, that is, returns in kind human attitudes and actions? And how can Buber who does not hesitate to chide theology for making statements about God, himself undertake the impossible and ascribe to Him mutuality in His partnership with man?

In spite of his very definite statements on the reciprocal I-Thou relation between God and man, Buber seems aware of the difficulty of his position. His difficulty, though, is probably no greater than that of any other believer. It is true, he says, that "the existence of mutuality

[74] See p. 24, *Supra*.

between God and man cannot be proved, just as God's existence cannot be proved. Yet he who dares speak of it, bears witness, and calls to witness him to whom he speaks—whether that witness is now or in the future."[75]

Nevertheless, Buber refuses to equate what he calls "bearing witness" with what is commonly called being religious. Recently asked about his religious views, he rejected the very term religion. Summing up decades of thinking, writing, and lecturing on the subject, he said:

> I must confess that I don't like religion very much, and I am very glad that in the Bible the word is not to be found. I even think that nothing in the world is as apt to mask the face of God as religion is, if it means religion instead of God. What the Bible says is not religious but holy. To be holy means simply to let everything in social, economic, political life be subjected to the kingship, the kingly rule of God.[76]

## 3. Encounter: Its Embodiment and Realization in Education

If all of life is to be subjected to the kingly rule of God, it must be the foremost concern of education to teach the young the meaning of this rule. Different ages have different images of what the educated man should be like. He may be "the Christian, the gentleman, the citizen," in accordance with the dominant idea of a particular period. Our society, though, seems to lack a well-defined educational ideal. The twentieth century, having destroyed many old values, has not yet created any new ones. We have no prototype after whom our youth might pattern itself. Buber, having lived through decades of crises and upheavals, says "But when all figures are shattered, when no figure is able any more to dominate and shape the present human material, what is there left to form? Nothing but the image of God."[77]

---

[75] Buber, "Postscript to I and Thou," *I and Thou*, p. 137.

[76] From an interview Martin Buber gave on BBC television, conducted by Rev. Vernon Sproxton, published in the BBC magazine *The Listener*, and reprinted in the *Saturday Review* of April 7, 1962.

[77] Buber, "Education," *Between Man and Man*, p. 102.

When Buber speaks of human material that must be formed in "the image of God," he does not speak of the need for a parochial nor even a generally "religious" education. He means that education, as all of life, must be governed by a principle of spirituality, by what he calls "the holy." The educator is charged with the awesome responsibility of shaping the human raw-material into truly human beings who understand the inter-relatedness of Creator, creature, and fellow-creature. Each new-born child represents, and in a certain sense really is, all of mankind—past, present and future. "In every hour the human race begins."[78]

Therefore the educational process must, to the largest possible degree, match in creativity the new creation, the child with whom it has to deal. It must be aware of the preciousness of newness, "this grace of beginning again and ever again."[79] The educator must not permit himself to get into a rut of routine-teaching. Ideally, teaching is an ever-renewed encounter between a mature Thou and a maturing I through which both teacher and student grow. For the teacher's substance is not diminished by his giving of it freely—it rather grows in proportion to what he "lands" of it to the student with whom he stands in an essential relation. And the student grows in human substance in proportion to what he receives from his teacher. Their encounter makes him into an "apostle," for he transmits its immediacy to all whom he meets, even if he never consciously repeats or "proclaims" what he was taught, not even his teacher's name. In this way, education of one individual or of one generation affects all future generations, and the educator becomes truly a creator.

However, unlike other creators, the educator cannot choose the material with and upon which he is going to work. The teacher entering a schoolroom is faced with an "indiscriminately flung together" group: the unattractive, the slow-witted, the lazy mixed with the attractive, the gifted, the eager ones. He cannot afford the luxury of selectivity, of rejecting the one element and accepting the Other, "for in the manifold variety of the children the variety of creation is placed before him."[80]

---

78 *Ibid.*, p. 83.

79 *Ibid.*

80 *Ibid.*, p. 95.

This variety of creation is a challenge to his own creative powers, as he must try and overcome the spiritual and emotional drabness of his classroom's "unerotic situation" by entering into an essential relation even with the unlovable and the undesirable.

A real teacher does not permit himself to let his personal inclination or disinclination affect his willingness to be available to any of his pupils. They are given to him as part of the world, and he will reciprocate by giving them a part in the world.

"The class before him is like a mirror of mankind, so multiform, so full of contradictions, so inaccessible."[81] The teacher, not having chosen his students, yet accepts them all, and in his acceptance he embraces them in their actual present as well as in their potential future being. He is stirred to discover on some of their faces a look that shows "the chaos preceding the cosmos of a real face."[82] To be able to assist them on their way from chaos to cosmos, he must have their confidence. But confidence is not simply given for the asking, nor can the teacher win it even by the best educational intention. Confidence develops out of the educational encounter in which the as yet unstable and often frightened I of the adolescent, possibly disappointed by an unreliable world, meets a Thou it can trust, a Thou that will not let down his insecure I. If the pupil has the feeling that the teacher really cares for and is concerned with him and his problems, he will even accept discipline which is as necessary as it is repugnant to a young person. Undergirding discipline with love in a sustained educational relation with his pupil, the teacher hopes that this discipline will eventually turn inward and, as self-discipline, become an integral part of the student's character rather than remain a shackling device forced upon him from the outside.

On cannot, in fact, educate by force or by imposition. Education must be understood as a process of subtle influence on the student and not as harsh interference with his natural growth. The best teacher educates "as though he did not,"[83] neither by intervention, nor "by ruse or subterfuge," but by almost imperceptible suggestion. Teaching not by compulsion but by communion, the educator not only avoids

81 Buber, "Education of Character," *Between Man and Man*, p. 112.

82 *Ibid*.

83 Buber, "Education," *Between Man and Man*, p. 90.

rebelliousness in the student, but he so enters the student's life that he can shape his personality, as it were, from within.

Buber uses the symbols of a funnel and a pump in comparing old and new educational methods. The old, authoritarian way of educating a student is to feed him information as through a funnel, while the modern way (which, though, would seem to be at least as old as the Socratic method) extracts knowledge from the student as by a pump. The pump-method helps the student to realize his own creative potential by drawing him out of himself, and by drawing him simultaneously into a relationship conducive to the development of his faculties to think and to set for himself.

The ideal way of learning would be not to study certain subjects in school under professional teachers, but to share, to whatever modest degree, in the work of a "master," be he philosopher or coppersmith, simply by living with him. The student or apprentice learns in and through such a life-situation not only his master's knowledge or skill, but he partakes of the master's "spirit." If modern education can re-create this atmosphere, the student will learn "how life is lived in the spirit, face to face with the Thou."[84]

Buber realizes that contemporary social conditions irrevocably call for specialization, and that a school system and professional teachers are an indispensable part of the kind of departmentalization without which our society could not function. But he wants education taken out of the It-world where it has become a "science of teaching," and to be infused instead with the Thou-spirit characteristic of the best tradition of the old master-apprentice relationship. "Education" as technical skill is just another subject to be taught in our professional schools. But education as encounter between teacher and student is a human relation which may possibly regain "the paradise of pure instinctiveness"[85] which it lost when it became objectified by specialization.

Teaching must soften the hard animal egotism of the young so that they can be bent in the direction of some concerns other than their own. The good teacher awakens in the student the inclination towards a Thou. At first this will probably be only the Thou he experiences in the

84 Buber, *I and Thou*, p. 42.

85 Buber, "Education," *Between Man and Man*, p. 90.

teacher. But gradually, the student must be led to experience the Thou of living knowledge, as well as the Thou of the demanding and giving world beyond the teacher's person. By learning gradually to confront the world as Thou, the student will gradually learn to confront himself as I.

It has been said that education opens for man a window into the world. Buber says, in effect, that the teacher opens for the pupil—and opens the pupil for—the world of Thou. The world of Thou as experienced in the educational process does not consist of a mere accumulation of information the student might look up in a library. Education as Buber understands it could be described as a process of "in-form-ation," in the Aristotelian meaning of the term. The as yet unshaped character of the student is given form by the repeated face-to-face encounter with the teacher through whose mediating personality the knowledge of the world is filtered. The teacher who is more than an instructor transmits to the student not just the data of knowledge, but he develops in him the ability to know, and to understand. Ability to know is basically an ability to care—to be interested and absorbed in, and to establish a relation to, something outside of oneself.

All encounter leads to and deepens knowledge.[86] The epistemological role of Buber's Thou has been compared to that of the sun in Plato's Republic.[87] The presence of the Thou in any encounter is the source of light by which the I can "see," that is know. But the presence of the teacher's Thou in a personal encounter with a student is of such ultimate importance for his acquisition of knowledge and for the formation of his character that it should take precedence over any other creative work the teacher might be engaged in: "... more powerful and more holy than all writing is the presence of a man who is simply and immediately present."[88]

The educator need not be perfect in order to be effective, nor need he be outstanding in any particular field. But he must be available to the student, not just for technical consultation, but as a human being who

86 See p. 15, *Supra*.

87 Emmanuel Levinas, galley proof of a forthcoming publication to be called *Martin Buber und die Erkenntnistheorie*.

88 Buber, "Productivity and Existence," *Pointing the Way*, p. 7.

responds to the needs of another human being. The simple and immediate presence of the teacher, his "being-there" as someone who will listen and to whom one can turn, creates in his student a feeling of trust upon which he can build all his other relations. "Trust, trust in the world, because this human being exists—that is the most inward achievement of the relation in education."[89] The existence of the trusted teacher gives meaning not only to the student's personal life, but it shows him that life as such is meaningful, and that learning and living are really the same. The teacher's being-there, his "truth-of-existence" becomes, for the child, "existence-of-truth."

But though the teacher-student encounter is as deeply personal as any meeting of I and Thou, it is not characterized by the full mutuality which Buber finds indispensable in most other dialogical relations. He asserts that a student cannot, and in fact must not reciprocate fully the "inclusion" (Umfassung) of his own personality by the teacher. An educational encounter "is based on a concrete but one-sided experience of inclusion."[90]

Inclusion is a non-physical embrace, a gathering up in one's own being the being of an Other whom one regards not "as a mere sum of qualities, strivings and inhibitions,"[91] but whom one enfolds in the "wholeness" of his personality. The educator who is in full control of the student, the educational situation, and of himself, consciously includes, that is experiences those three factors in the process of teaching. But "... the pupil cannot experience the educating of the educator. The educator stands on both ends of the common situation, the pupil only at one end."[92] If the student crossed over to where the teacher stands, and if he experienced the teacher "from over there," the educational relationship would be terminated. It would, instead, turn into friendship, with both sides practicing inclusion of the Other.

Encounter is marked by full mutuality only when the partners meet, as it were, on the same level. Such an encounter "happens;" it is

---

89 Buber, "Education," *Between Man and Man*, p. 98.

90 *Ibid.*, p. 99.

91 Buber, "Postscript to I and Thou," *I and Thou*, p. 132.

92 Buber, "Education," *Between Man and Man*, p. 100.

unplanned, and comes about by grace.[93] But if one partner must work upon the other, he must of necessity stand somewhat above the person he wants to influence. The very purposiveness of their meeting makes real reciprocity impossible. (This holds true also for all "healing through meeting," that is for an encounter of psycho-therapist and patient, or of pastor and parishioner.) The effectiveness of a purposive or professional encounter is undermined if the partners do not recognize its special character and keep at a certain distance from each other.

While Buber always stresses the need for "unreserved" in any dialogical relation (which would, in fact, lose its dialogical nature if the partners held back from each other anything essential), a purposive encounter must be guided by the principle of reserve. The active partner must judge carefully how much and when to give, and what to withhold from the "submissive" partner, who, though, must not be permitted to become passive. For the effectiveness of any, even a modified, dialogical relation depends to a large degree on the active participation of both partners.

It is difficult but necessary to maintain the delicate balance between intimacy and detachment in a not fully dialogical situation. The teacher (as well as the therapist or pastor) must find a workable mid-position between the cold neutrality of the professional and the emotional over-involvement of the dilettante, for neither of these extreme attitudes would permit him to do his work well. The student (or patient or parishioner) will be open to the beneficial influence of the Thou he encounters in proportion to the respect he feels for the Thou's human authority, and this respect is experienced best where a certain distance—though never remoteness—is kept. The teacher, therefore, remaining on his side of the educational encounter, must reach out to the student "over there" and draw him near in inclusion. But he must avoid identification with the student which might result in a telescoping of their respective positions, and in an end of his effectiveness as educator.

Buber warns against confusing inclusion with empathy. An act of empathy leads to loss of identity, because it causes an individual to absorb the "reality" (that is the personality-plus-setting) of another to

93 See p. 17, *Supra*.

such an extent that it destroys both Other's and his own separate being. For a self, empathically transporting itself into an Other, lives the Other's self from the inside out, to the exclusion of its own concreteness. But "inclusion is the opposite of this. It is the extension of one's own concreteness."[94] It is that "experiencing the other side" on which all encounter is based,[95] the "making present" to oneself the reality of the Other. Including but not absorbing the other side, the teacher does not assimilate the pupil's personality; he liberates and strengthens it.

The act of inclusion provides a certain counter-balance to the arbitrariness inherent in the educator's selection of subjects to be taught. For taking into account all factors which make up the student's personality and the uniqueness of a particular educational situation somewhat limits the subjectivity of the teacher's presentation of the educational material. To choose this material, to select out of an almost limitless store of possible knowledge that section judged to be most relevant to the life of a student or a generation of students is one of the most difficult tasks facing education in general and the individual educator in particular. "The forces of the world which the child needs for the building up of his substance must be chosen by the educator from the world and drawn into himself. ... The educator educates himself to be their vehicle."[96] The student's character and his attitude towards the world are affected decisively by the way in which this world percolates through the teacher's personality, a fact of which the perceptive teacher must be constantly aware in his dealings with the child.

The educational encounter is not an end in itself, but serves to make the young person aware of his inter-relatedness with the world, its people and their culture. Education, of course, is not limited to the home or the classroom. The child is educated by any of the endlessly many things he encounters in his environment, and his "character is formed by the interpenetration of all those multifarious, opposing

94 Buber, "Education," *Between Man and Man*, p. 97.

95 See p. 57, *Supra*.

96 Buber, "Education," *Between Man and Man*, p. 101.

influences,"[97] even if those influences are barely noticed because they seem so peripheral and insignificant.

But the educational fringe-benefits of incidental experiences, important though they are, must be augmented by the educational relation between teacher and pupil which is lifted out of the realm of chance. The teacher, realizing that he is only one element among the other "form-giving forces" to which the child is exposed, sets out purposefully to acquaint the student with those subjects of knowledge which seem best suited to achieve the pre-determined educational goal. To educate purposefully means to pronounce a double value-judgment: first, by selecting a certain curriculum; and second, by trying to develop in the student a feeling for right and wrong.

But this must be done by patient instruction and constructive criticism rather than by imposing upon the student the teacher's own moral concepts. "To dictate what is good and evil in general is not his business,"[98] says Buber rather brusquely. In accordance with his often-voiced aversion against universals, and in spite of speaking of "eternal values" and "eternal norm" in a different context,[99] he suggests that the teacher avoid general statements on some abstract good and evil. He should, instead, simply answer a concrete question concerning a given situation by pointing out the right and wrong as it applies to that particular situation.

It would seem, though, that Buber limits the role of education almost fatally by this suggestion. A good teacher certainly never "dictates" to a student what he should or should not do. But if all education is basically "education of character," as Buber maintains, if it is the molding (*Bildung*) of an I through meeting a Thou, it must surely set itself the task of inculcating in the young a sense of moral values "in general." It may then be education's additional task to warn the young person of the dangers of doctrinal rigidity, and to teach him that there are some issues so complicated and ambivalent as to demand a very special consideration which may have to go "beyond good and evil," or

97 Buber, "Education of Character," *Between Man and Man*, p. 106.

98 *Ibid.*, p. 107.

99 *Ibid.*, p. 116.

rather, which may defy a clear-cut definition of what is good or evil in that particular instant.

Buber's recurrent demand that man answer the need of the hour "quantum satis"[100] is justified on a pragmatic level, that is, whenever a satisfactory solution for a special problem must be found. But it should not be made into an educational principle. A real teacher must surely be more than an advisor-on-the-spot. Counseling the young in a given problematic situation is an educator's legitimate task. But beyond that task of the moment lies the long-range task of preparing the child to know how to deal with the next "concrete situation"—not by waiting until it arises, but by teaching him that there are certain universally applicable moral laws. An unformed young mind needs the assurance of knowing that there is indeed a morally right and a wrong way of behavior, even if the absoluteness of such a statement may occasionally have to be modified.

But how can a teacher exert an influence upon the student without imposing his own will and his own view upon him? By creating, Buber contends, in the student a disposition towards what the teacher has found to be right within himself. Teaching is fundamentally an "existential communion" between an individual who is in actual being, and an Other who is in the process of becoming, with the one who is helping the Other to be. The teacher sees in the young person committed to his care a promise that he may turn into a personality, preciously unique, who will become "the bearer of a special task of existence which can be fulfilled through him and through him alone."[101] Education is a process guiding the young person towards a realization that he has such a task, and of assisting him in unfolding "… the primal power which has scattered itself and still scatters itself, in all human beings in order that it may grow up in each man in the special form of that man."[102]

The educator need not be an extra-ordinary person in order to render this assistance to the student, but he must be a real person. The integrity

---

100 See p. 52, *Supra*.

101 Buber, "Elements of the Interhuman," *Psychiatry*, p. 111.

102 *Ibid*.

of his personality will affect the student more than any conscious and formal teaching would.

Buber juxtaposes education and propaganda as two different ways of affecting man's view and his attitude towards life. Education is concerned with man as an individual whose human potential should be actualized. Propaganda, however, is interested only in using him as a means to achieve its own ends. It indoctrinates him with slogans rather than educates him to think for himself. For the ability to think makes man independent; but propaganda wants to capture and subjugate rather than to liberate the human mind. While the educator believes in teaching through meeting, and in transmitting knowledge through the mediation of his own person, the propagandist relies on the mechanized devices of loudspeaker and television screen to advertise a cause in whose rightness he himself does not quite believe. For if he did believe in it, he would not abolish the human factor, that is personal encounter, as a means to bring about its realization. Propaganda is "sublimated violence," namely the violence done to an Other by an overriding of his personal convictions, and by an utter disregard for his uniqueness as a human being.

The methods used by propaganda to influence men are to be rejected unequivocally. But, asks Buber, should one also reject as undesirable the influence an educator may exert upon his students by letting his own "Weltanschauung" color his teaching? Buber feels that a subjective presentation of the educational material is to be welcomed. A teacher can transmit knowledge, that is "the world," only as he sees it. If he did not read a text or interpret a historical event from his own point of view, he would lack the personal involvement necessary for a fruitful educational relationship. Teaching is as subjective as is all living, and personal value-judgments are not only unavoidable, but they are desirable in an educational encounter.

However, in addition to taking a personal stand and letting the student know about it, the educator must also be able to look "behind" a text or an event for its meaning. Education must help the student to develop a view of the world, and not just a world-view. "Weltanschauung" defines man's goal in a certain way, and points out the road towards this goal. But the goal itself is to see the world in its totality, and not under this or that slant. To be educated means to be able to distinguish between appearance and reality, between "seeming" and "being"; it is to be a genuine person, and to live authentically.

The truly educated man whose mind is well-formed and not only well informed need not be neutral in matters of opinion, nor superficially "tolerant" of the views of others. Though he may and in fact ought to be outspoken about his own beliefs, he must be able to acknowledge the legitimacy of divergent ones. He must recognize that mankind, in spite of its common roots, branched out in different directions and developed different sets of values. Education must work towards man's common exploration of their common ground, in affirmation of their mutual involvement in mankind.

As the educational encounter derives its significance from the teacher's inclusion of his student with all his positive and negative personality traits, so education as such must practice inclusion of all the constructive forces of the world and mould in and through them the student's character. "The constructive forces are eternally the same: they are the world bound up in community, turned to God."[103]

## 4. Encounter: Its Embodiment and Realization in Society

The words, "the world bound up in community, turned to God," might serve not only as a definition of Buber's educational goal, but also as a summarization of his social philosophy. As all of his thought, Buber's social views are religiously motivated, and grounded in his conviction that man-with-man is the source as well as the goal of all "genuine" living. But can the principle man-with-man, significantly stated in the singular, be applied to the life of man with men, that is, to the plurality of society?

Buber contends that society (Gesellschaft) is a lifeless construct as long as it is merely an association of individuals. In order to become an organic structure, it must be built on and around the I-Thou principle. In fact, mankind's very survival depends on a reduction from the plurality of an internally unrelated composite to the singularity of a

103 Buber, "Education of Character," *Between Man and Man*, p. 101.

dialogically inter-related community (*Gemeinschaft*) of "human persons."

Buber's social philosophy is an attempt to re-direct man—not towards a far-away Utopian ideal, but towards his fellow-man. Men, he says, has developed two kinds of "vision of rightness": a messianic eschatology which is perfection in time, and a social Utopia which is perfection in space. "Eschatology means perfection of creation; Utopia the unfolding of the possibilities, latent in mankind's communal life, of a 'right order.'"[104] In eschatology, "the decisive act happens from above,"[105] beyond the realm of human endeavor, in some time-to-come. But Utopia need not be located in the future. The "right order" can be translated into reality by the "conscious human will" setting to work in and on the here and now. In order to do this work, society which is now no more than "an aggregate of essentially unrelated individuals ... held together by a 'political,' i.e., a coercive principle of government" must be re-structured; "it must be built up of little societies on the bases of communal life and of the associations of all these societies."[106]

Buber sees as prototype of such "little societies" the Jewish agricultural communal settlements in Israel. He feels that these "kibbutzim" represent at least "an experiment that did not fail,"[107] if not yet a signal success, in regenerating and rebuilding society from within. As cooperatives which are based on collective ownership of all property and on collective organization of all work, the *kibbutzim* are governed by the general assembly of all members who share the responsibility for the physical and cultural needs and all social services of the commune. Though Buber stresses the fact that the *kibbutzim* still have to do much re-thinking of their ideologies and much re-forming of their reforms, he looks upon them as likely nuclei of an evolving commonwealth which will be an organic "community of communities."

A community, Buber holds, cannot be founded. It must grow as "a living togetherness; constantly renewing itself ... (in) the immediacy of

104 Martin Buber, "The Utopian Element in Socialism," *Paths in Utopia*, trans. R.F.C. Hull (Boston: Beacon Press, 1958), p. 8.

105 *Ibid.*

106 Buber, "Marx and the Renewal of Society," *Paths in Utopia*, p. 80.

107 Buber, "Epilogue," *Paths in Utopia*, pp. 139 ff.

relationships."[108] He realizes, however, that this is difficult under present-day conditions. The community spirit which characterized older and simpler societies is irrevocably gone. The modern city has no *Agora,* and modern society has replaced the dialogue between man and man with negotiations carried on by its elected representatives. The I-Thou relation seems to suffocate under "the pressure of numbers" exerted by today's political and economic forces which are interested only in membership and in quantity, but not in the "living togetherness" of human persons.

Analyzing contemporary society, Buber finds that modern life is not determined by the unifying principle of community, but by the alienating principle of division. There are divisions of all kinds between man and man, between man and the world, and even between man and himself. "The day is cleanly divided, and the soul, too."[109] Modern man, rent by a fragmentation of interests and concerns, is a disintegrated man, just as modern society is a disintegrated society. Both lack "unity of being," by which Buber does not mean "a static unity of the uniform, but the great dynamic unity of the multiform."[110] The family is still a vestige of the integrated, organic community of earlier times, but its existence, too, is threatened by the crisis in which contemporary society finds itself.

How can this crisis be overcome: by pronouncing, Buber advises, the "essential We" which will re-crate the small, integrated, organic community and contribute to the creation of the large, but equally integrated and organic community of communities. The essential We, Buber explains, does not fit into any "current sociological categories." It is "a community of several persons, who have reached a self and self-responsibility,"[111] and it is characterized by the essential relations connecting its members. Only men who can "truly" say Thou to one another can truly say We with and of one another. The essential We is not simply the plural form of any given number of I's. Just as the unrelated individual is not a Thou, but a He or She, as "the nameless,

---

108 Buber, "In the Midst of Crisis," *Paths in Utopia,* p. 135.

109 Buber, "In the Midst of Crisis," *Paths in Utopia,* p. 136.

110 Buber, "Education of Character," *Between Man and Man,* p. 116.

111 Buber, "What is Man?" *Between Man and Man,* p. 175.

faceless crowd" in which this He or She is "entangled" as a stranger among strangers is not a "We" but "the one" (das Man).

Buber discusses the fact that both Kierkegaard and Heidegger deal with the anonymous aggregate of men who have no authentic existence because they lack a sense of personal uniqueness and personal destiny. What should be the salience of their individual existence is leveled off into the undistinguished and undistinguishable flatness of a mass-existence. For Kierkegaard, the crowd is "untruth"; only when man, refusing to become conditioned by the crowd-mediocrity, breaks away to become a Single One, does he confront the unconditioned truth of God. Disengaging himself from the crowd, Kierkegaard's Single One renounces also all personal, that is essential, relations[112] until he stands "alone before God," in dread and anxiety.

Heidegger's man, on the other hand, "stands before himself and nothing else, and—since in the last resort one cannot stand before oneself—he stands in his anxiety and dread before nothing."[113] Buber shares Kierkegaard's and Heidegger's view that a crowd-determined life lacks authenticity. In order to live in and with truth, "you must," he says, "not be governed by the crowd. You must ... 'unmass it' as far as you can."[114] But he does not conclude, as they do, that existential dread is a necessary concomitant of a life lived in authenticity. For Buber, man who liberates himself from the "unfreedom" of the crowd becomes free for something else—for the essential We of true community which "throws a bridge from self-being to self-being across the abyss of dread of the universe."[115]

The spirit of the essential We arises in a "transient form" on special occasions, when men draw together in the face of a catastrophe. The death of a mutually beloved person, or a danger threatening a group may open one man to the Other as their common experience melts away their usual reservedness. Their life is then suddenly marked by a sense of purpose and by an "incandescence" it never had before.

---

112 See p. 69, *Supra*.

113 Buber, "What is Man?" *Between Man and Man*, p. 172.

114 From an interview Buber gave on BBC Television, reprinted in *Saturday Review* of April 7, 1962.

115 Buber, "What is Man?" *Between Man and Man*, p. 175.

But it should not take catastrophes to create the essential We. The essential We, as all dialogic, should be a sustained attitude rather than the result of some chance occasion. Whenever and wherever the essential We is understood and accepted as man's mandate of man, it will lift him out of the inner uneventfulness and deadening monotony of a crowd-existence. Pronouncing the essential We is a human event in which man discovers self-being through being-with-an Other, that is, through community.

The community of the essential We in its "constant form" develops, for instance, through working in the lowest strata of society, among the uneducated and the poor. Such work is marked by, or indeed is "a sacrificial realization of faith" in every-day life which is accepted in its "simple, unexalted, unselected reality ... just as it is."[116] The essential We is a positive statement of I and Thou, with no trace of meekness or self-abnegation. Yet it lacks the loud self-assertiveness of vanity and of lust for power—and therefore it cannot be found in political parties.

Buber is gravely concerned with the influence of the "party" or the "collective" which according to him enslaves people everywhere. He feels that "the parties and party-like groups in the so-called democracies"[117] have their members in as authoritarian a grip, and that they exert as much pressure upon them, as do the ideological collectives in the totalitarian countries. Each collective appropriates to itself supreme authority over its members, while none any longer recognizes "any universal sovereignty in idea, faith or spirit."[118] No personal appeal is possible against the decrees and decisions of the collective which has become a Moloch devouring in its "fiery jaws" the individual's selfhood.

Claiming his total loyalty, the collective does not even permit man to remain loyal to himself as an independent, free spirit.

Nor can the individual pledge himself to the "cause" of a collective, though he thinks that he does. But in reality he has no self to pledge, for he surrenders it completely to the group. By destroying man as man, the "collectivity" of party, state, or any other ideologically exclusive

116 Buber, "In the Midst of Crisis," *Paths in Utopia*, p. 132.

117 Buber, "Education of Character," *Between Man and Man*, p. 110.

118 *Ibid.*

organization also destroys man-with-man, that is the communal spirit necessary for building and maintaining a healthy society. Paradoxically, joining a group isolates man from man, for it eliminates the "ontic directness which is the decisive presupposition of the I-Thou relation."[119]

Without an I-Thou relation, however, man is without truth. The crowd with its lack of inner relatedness may not be, as Kierkegaard maintained, untruth, but it seems to Buber to be non-truth. Therefore man must find a way to extend the truth of dialogic living into the realm of public life. "I think it is essential that a man should not only have truth in his private life, but as a member of his party, too."[120]

If man succeeds in applying the I-Thou principle to public life, he creates a community which Buber defines as a union of many lives lived towards each other. Community furthers an individual's personal growth, and benefits from it. But contemporary society tends to mistake collectivity for community, though "collectivity is not a binding but a bundling together ... based on an organized atrophy of personal existence."[121] In a collective, men are not turned towards each other—they simply march or work side by side. But in a community, man is turned towards man in "a dynamic facing of, the Other, a flowing from I to Thou."[122]

The collective supplants the need for personal decisions with obedience to its own rules and regulations. Living by directives handed down to him, man is apt either not to develop his own sense of direction, or else to lose it; and being relived of personal responsibilities, he does not know how to respond to the "speech" of the world whose word does not seem any longer to address him personally. The

119 Buber, "What is Man?" *Between Man and Man,* p. 176. There seems to be a remarkable inconsistency between Buber's strong opposition of ideologically oriented, collective living and his equally strong affirmation of Israel's *kibbutzim* which, as he must surely know, are plagued by many of the problems he criticizes as objectionable concomitants of "party" or "party-like" organizations.

120 From an interview Buber gave on BBC Television, reprinted in *Saturday Review* of April 7, 1962.

121 Buber, "Dialogue," *Between Man and Man,* p. 31.

122 *Ibid.*

collective replaces that world, as it replaces a personal search for truth with political and ideological platforms and programs.

In the modern collective—that is, according to Buber, in much of today's society—there is neither monologue, nor dialogue. Man has become silent, even as he joins the chorus of those who shout political slogans.

Buber is concerned not only with the loss of personal responsibility through collective living, but also with the still more serious loss of man's responsiveness to the voice of God whose word alone gives life and meaning to the world. If man, for whatever reasons, ceases to respond to and address his Eternal Thou, all his efforts to create an essential We will fail. For true community arises only when men enter into a twofold relations: to each other, and with and through each Other to God, their mutual "living Center."

Young people are particularly susceptible to the lure of the collective because they feel, perhaps unconsciously, that there is security in numbers. Collective living alleviates their fear to be left to their own inner devices. They are afraid of having "to rely on themselves, on a self which no longer receives its direction from eternal values,"[123] for their dialogue with God, if ever they had time to cultivate it at all, has lapsed into a stammer, or into complete silence. Unable to discern in the bewildering multiformity of life a master-form in which to mould their souls, they escape into the uniformity of collective living.

Collectivity breeds two kinds of inertia: man loses, or has no chance to develop, the initiative and drive that life in an open society necessitates; and, much worse, he soon begins to suffer from a human inertia. For a system which discourages the development of individual personality produces man so disinterested in others as persons that they neither give nor expect to receive any human recognition.

While Buber criticizes collectivity-induced inertia, he deplores even more the inertia of man who, though he lives in a free society, is without concern for the common weal, and gives in to the human tendency to leave the problems and responsibilities of the world to others. To consider social responsibilities a burden to be avoided rather than an appreciated privilege is a tragic waste of a unique opportunity

---

[123] Buber, "Education of Character," *Between Man and Man*, p. 115.

for meaningful living. "Life lived in freedom is personal responsibility or it is a pathetic farce."[124]

Calling for man's personal involvement in the affairs of the world, Buber says to him, in effect: "Tua res agitur." Each man's interest is at stake—not in a narrowly selfish sense, but in the sense of personal survival through group survival. Any human institution has only as much spirit and meaning as man is willing to give to it. If contemporary society seems at times so over-mechanized as to be devoid of human values, it is man's task to re-vitalize it by re-vitalizing his dialogical relations. He must try and counter-act society's disregard of human and spiritual values and its over-emphasis on non-essentials by saying Thou to his fellow-man, so that together, in mutual responsibility, they can encounter the world and its problems as an essential We.

But contemporary man finds it almost impossible to be a living part of an essential We, for, having lost direct contact with God and man, he is beset by "cosmic insecurity." To compensate for this loss, he snatches at the doubtful support of a pseudo-security provided by the indirect contacts of group-living. Yet the future can be built neither by insecure individuals, nor by pseudo-secure collectivists, but only by securely-anchored man-with-man.

Buber thinks that modern individualism is just as destructive a social force as is modern collectivism. Both are expressions of the same human condition: "cosmic and social homelessness, dread of the universe and dread of life, resulting in an existential constitution of solitude."[125] The individualist, thinking of himself as an unconnected monad, accepts what he considers his cosmic exposure and isolation as his fate. He saves himself from existential despair by glorifying it. The collectivist tries to escape his destiny of solitude by total immersion in the group. The more "massive" the group formation, the greater is his relief at having been saved.

The collective reduces, devaluates, and desecrates all personal relationships because, as shown before, they interfere actually or potentially with a member's loyalty to his group. And by foreclosing all possibility of meeting a Thou, the collective successfully prevents man

124 Buber, "Education of Character," *Between Man and Man*, p. 92.

125 Buber, "What is Man?" *Between Man and Man*, p. 200.

from encountering himself as an I. But the individualist is not an I either. For though he pointedly asserts man's particular being, the individualist really has no being at all, because true being is relatedness.[126] Therefore the much-stressed I of the individualist is fictitious.

Collectivism, says Buber, understands man only as a part of a group which masks man's face so that his humanity cannot be seen any more at all. And individualism understands only part of man, that is man-in-relation-to-himself, which is a distortion of his face. But one can see the true face of man and his role in society "by beginning neither with the individual nor with the collectivity, but only with the reality of the mutual relation between man and man."[127]

A society founded on the dialogical principle is a society which recognizes the worth and dignity of the human person. Buber, admittedly appropriating a Kantian postulate, warns against using men as means, as material with which to set up the intricate mechanism of modern civilization. Men are ends in themselves, not to be used, but to be understood in their distinct being.

Indifference to an individual's personality is typical of the It-world which evaluates a man's effectiveness alone, without regard for his human qualities. Similarly, the It of collective living is interested exclusively in the performance of the group, and in its success or failure to achieve its ideological goals. The group-members are, as it were, banded together for assault, and must not be distracted from the singleness of their purpose by any internal dialogical relations. Pursuing the goal of achieving a higher form of society, the group disdains to see this goal partially achieved within itself, by personal attachments between an I and a Thou. The collective is so concerned with the betterment of humanity that it wants to waste neither time nor effort on the betterment of man. "The opinion apparently is that the man who whiles away his time as a guest on an oasis may be accounted lost for the project of irrigating the Sahara."[128]

---

126 See pp. 14, *Supra*.

127 Buber, "Forward," *Between Man and Man*, p. xi.

128 Buber, "Dialogue," *Between Man and Man*, p. 31.

As long as society looks upon the individual not in the immediacy of his personal being, but through the medium of his job-performance, as long as it sees in him a functionary and an operator rather than a human being, it will remain a humanly arid wasteland in which "the personal human being ceases to be the living member of a social body and becomes a cog in the 'collective' machine."[129]

Technology, as Buber is well aware, steps up the efficiency of the worker's performance. Yet a man who "performs" a task approaches it in the It-attitude; he plays a role. Only when man approaches a task in the Thou-attitude is he really integrated in his work which becomes a living action sustained by, and in turn sustaining his entire personality. Industrial society has streamlined man's life, but at the cost of taking it out of the life-stream of essential relations.

Buber is afraid that we are so out of touch, in human terms, with one another that we may soon reach the stage "of making ourselves understood only by means of the dictograph, that is, without contact with one another."[130] This lack of contact is alarming because man's chance for human growth and society's chance for becoming a true community is increased or diminished in proportion to the degree of directness with which men relate themselves to one another. It is true that neither the individual nor society can completely dispense with the It. Contemporary life is unthinkable without mechanization and automation. But at least some of the triviality of the It can be redeemed, and the machine can, to some extent, be ensouled if "the presence of the Thou moves like the spirit upon the face of the waters."[131] To abjure this spirit, says Buber, is to abjure life.

Man must not permit the It-world to overwhelm him with a feeling that the individual is powerless to affect a change in the sociological and political pattern of his time. He must not ask dispiritedly and vaguely what one can do about it all, but spiritedly and concretely: what do I have to do? The answer will then be equally concrete:

> You shall not withhold yourself. You, imprisoned in the shells in which society, state, church, school, economy, public opinion,

---

129 Buber, "In the Midst of Crisis," *Paths in Utopia*, p. 132.

130 Buber, "Distance and Relation," *Psychiatry*, p. 102.

131 Buber, *I and Thou*, p. 48.

> and your own pride have stuck you, indirect one among indirect ones, break through your shells, become direct; man, have contact with men![132]

To "become direct" means, for Buber, to become dialogically and immediately related to an Other—not by having an occasional social contact with him, but by living in an "unbroken world of Thou" in which "the isolated moments of relation are bound in a life of world solidarity" (Weltleben der Verbundenheit).[133]

Buber sees in the creation of an "unbroken world of Thou" the only solution to the problems troubling contemporary society. In the power struggle of individualism versus collectivism, man is asked to choose between two false alternatives. But Buber's social philosophy presents man with a third alternative: the life of dialogue. The narrow ridge of the Interhuman where the I encounters the Thou has no room for either one of the false alternatives. But it is the creative realm of "the genuine third alternative" where "the life decision of future generations" will be made. It is the potential birthplace of "the genuine person" who will "establish genuine community."[134]

Only this third alternative of men's communion with and mutual responsibility for each other has a truly human character. Animals may live either by themselves, or in groups. "The gorilla, too, is an individual, a termitary, too, is a collective, but I and Thou exist only in our world, because man exists, and the I, moreover, exists only through the relation to the Thou."[135]

However, contemporary man, Buber thinks, finds it particularly hard to relate himself to a Thou. Going through a "crisis of speech" which started in World War I, he suffers from an incapacity for genuine dialogue, regardless of who his potential partner might be. It is difficult for him, for instance, to pray, that is to address God, even if he believes in His existence. Nor can he really address his fellow-man, for he has lost his simple trust in the Other's genuineness. Our age is characterized by "universal mistrust" which rules the world like a demon. This is not

---

132 Buber, "Politics, Community, and Peace," *Pointing the Way*, p. 109.

133 Buber, *I and Thou*, p. 100.

134 Buber, "What is Man?" *Between Man and Man*, pp. 205.

135 *Ibid.*

man's "primal mistrust" of the outsider, the stranger, the one with different ways. Rather, it is the sick distrust in the true existence of the Other, his human-ness, his dialogical accessibility, his Thou-potential. Modern man not only fears the Other because of his otherness, as ancient man did. Modern man presupposes that his fellow-man is untrustworthy, that one must be on guard against him, and that one must try to see through and unmask him.

Only an overcoming of mistrust and a "rebirth of dialogue" between man and man holds any hope for the future. Buber makes it clear that genuine dialogue is as little "an uncritical acceptance of man's statements" based on "a vague idealism" as it is the wish to "see through" or to "unmask" them.[136] Rather, it is an expression of trust which must, however, not be blind, but clear-sighted. Dialogical man's intention ought to be not to see through the Other, but simply to see him as he is; not to unmask, but to understand him, and to deal with him accordingly.

This is as true for a dialogue between individuals as it is true for a dialogue between ideological camps into which society is split. As long as they are only a substitute and cover-up for human beings, "a genuine word cannot arise between the camps."[137] But those human beings on both sides who have not yet been inauthenticated by collective living must choose genuinely human representatives who will speak for them, and to each other. Those representatives must not be politicians, "bound by the sin of the hours."[138] Their authority should be that of the spirit, their vision "the rescue of man." Considering the true needs of man for a human life in both camps, they should "unrelentingly distinguish between truth and propaganda," and "think with one another in terms of the whole planet."[139]

Thinking with and towards an Other will, Buber realizes, not eliminate legitimate differences in outlook. But he hopes that it will lead to a human arbitration, and therefore to an overcoming of the conflicts

---

136 Buber, "Hope for this Hour," *Pointing the Way*, p. 227.

137 Buber, "Genuine Dialogue and the Possibilities of Peace," *Pointing the Way*, p. 238.

138 *Ibid.*

139 *Ibid.*, p. 228.

of today's ideological camps. The success of this arbitration will depend not on the diplomatic skill, but on the good will and unreserved honesty of men willing and able to overcome their "camp"-bred antagonisms long enough to speak to each other.

The crisis of speech has marked five decades of hot and cold war, but "war has not produced this crisis; it is, rather, the crisis of man which has brought forth the total war and the unreal peace which followed.[140] War is a consequence of the cessation of "speech" between people who have lost the redeeming power of the human "word."

> But when the word has become entirely soundless, and on this side and on that soundlessly bears into the hearts of man the intelligence that no human conflict can really be resolved through killing, not even through mass killing, then the human word has already begun to silence the cannonade.[141]

However, Buber refuses to equate this human word with the deliberations of top-level international conferences which lack candor and true dialogical spirit. There can be no "rebirth of dialogue" unless and until there is a rebirth of the human spirit. Buber is therefore much less interested in a war of ideologies between nations, camps, or individuals than in a war of society against the "anti-human" spirit in its own midst.

The "counter-human" or "sub-human" element to be found in all societies profits from any "divisions" between people, and therefore over-emphasizes them. Buber calls this element "Satan" (which is the Hebrew designation of a hinderer). The satanical force of the anti-human tries to hinder or to prevent man from realizing that any division presents not only a separating partition, but also a connecting boundary between two entities. But the human solution to the human dilemma of the irrefutable existence of divisions is "to bear this division in common," to trust in man's humanity in spite of his often and painfully demonstrated inhumanity, and to "release speech from its ban."[142]

---

140 Buber, "Genuine Dialogue and the Possibilities of Peace," *Pointing the Way*, p. 236.

141 *Ibid*.

142 *Ibid*., pp. 238–239.

Buber's suggested solution certainly is human, but whether it is also realistic is doubtful. The global scope of foreign policy almost automatically rules out the direct approach from man to man which Buber advocates. And while one must share his hope that the representatives of the people, on the national and on the international scene, be men of vision and of integrity, one cannot quite believe that they will not have to be "bound by the aim of the hour," or by partisan considerations. Moreover, the vastly complex problems besetting mankind today may quite possibly resist being solved by being talked over, no matter how human nor how trusting the "speech." Open communication is obviously the most important precondition for arriving at an understanding between hostile camps. But "trust" alone may prove woefully inadequate in arbitrating some of the current diametrically opposed and therefore inescapably clashing world-views. Men of good will are certainly needed—but so are the most skillful diplomacy and statesmanship. Ingenious negotiations, much as Buber disdains them, may, at times, open the only way out of a deadlocked situation, and thereby create a modus vivendi for the present, if admittedly not the most desirable society of the future.

Buber evidently does not share the bitter frustration of today's "man in the street" which stems from the realization that his life is indeed "more and more determined by circumstances" which are utterly beyond his control, and beyond his dialogical reach. The man in the street is frightened by the disproportion between the unavoidable slowness of the democratic process—by which alone he can hope to make his voice heard—and the urgency with which crisis after crisis must be overcome. Simple men everywhere, with their universal needs, loves and fears have always felt that there would be no wars, if only they could talk things over with other simple men across the line dividing their respective camps. But it seems that the ever more intricate machinery of international relations and Buber's concept of an I-Thou encounter with its essential relations cancel each other out.

Buber, himself, however, anticipates a challenge to his request for a life of dialogue—not so much in the realm of opposing ideologies or politics, as within an industrial society whose working and living conditions are admittedly not conclusive to a deepening of personal relations between men. He realizes that he may be charged with unworldliness for suggesting an I-Thou encounter as a means for saving mankind from mutual exploitation and mutual psychical if not physical destruction. He imagines his challenger to say that such an encounter "takes place in the never-never land, not in the social context of the world in which we spend our days, and by which if by anything our reality is defined."[143]

How, asks Buber along with his fictitious opponent, can the "sacramental" happen, how can the "holy" word Thou be spoken in a big city office, or at the conveyor belt? How can the president of a large industrial enterprise "respond" to one man among thousands of anonymous workers? How can a philosophy of dialogue persist in its postulate that man experience the ever-changing existential situations he encounters in a deeply personal way, in view of the indisputable fact that he finds himself in a never-changing situation of depersonalization?

In reply, Buber points out, first, that he does not request, postulate, or demand a life of dialogue. Dialogue must happen—one cannot ask for it.[144] Secondly, the individual can fully regain his now impaired faculty for dialogue, in spite of all obstacles which modern life puts in the way of an I-Thou encounter, if he will not permit himself to become dehumanized by the complexities of a mechanized society. Also, he must not regard the life of dialogue as one of "spiritual luxuriousness," for even the lowliest man can open his heart and speak to an Other.

The worker in the factory, the laborer in the field, the minor, the store- or office-clerk—all of them may be inarticulate and quite inept at making conversation, let alone engage in a discussion, "that curious sport" of "breaking apart."[145] But their "modesty in communicating" is due to awkwardness, not to "stingy taciturnity."[146] For they know how to draw each other close—by a smile or by a handshake which is their form of genuine dialogue.

---

143 Buber, "Dialogue," *Between Man and Man*, p. 34.

144 But he does ask for it. See, as just one quote out of many throughout his work, pp. 110, *Supra*.

145 Buber, "Dialogue," *Between Man and Man*, p. 3.

146 Buber, "Politics, Community and Peace," *Pointing the Way*, p. 109.

In one way or another, all men, high and low alike, are worn down by the grind of unrelieved toil. Dulled by the deadly boredom of mechanization and subdued by the necessity of making a living, they are the prisoners of their own, seemingly inescapable routines. What modern man needs, says Buber, is a break-through—not into an extraordinary realm of heroics and excitement, but into the very ordinary realm of the simply human.

The simply human dimension of life is created (as has been shown before) by the dialogical spirit in which man encounters the world and his fellow-man. The voice of I and Thou can be heard even in the "clanking routine," if men will not use the perfunctoriness of their "shift" or the drabness of their setting as an excuse for their spiritual and emotional deaf-muteness. No place or time need be outside the province of I and Thou.

> No factory and no office is so abandoned by creation that a creative glance could not fly up from one working-place to another, from desk to desk, a sober and brotherly glance which guarantees the reality of creation which is happening—quantum satis.[147] And nothing is so valuable a service of dialogue between God and man as such an unsentimental and preserved exchange of glances between two men in an alien place.[148]

Genuine humanity, radiating from man to man, transforms even the most alien into a warmly familiar place, and creates in both men a feeling of belonging which eases the weight of their workload. As the individual does not have to wait for an exceptional occasion to give and receive his modest bit of warmth and fellowship, so society does not have to wait for sweeping reforms to reinstate its members as human persons. Any two people sharing the same time and space can also share their common humanity through an I-Thou encounter. And society can be rebuilt from within—if and when it succeeds in transfiguring punch card-holders into men and women.

It is true that the president of a large corporation cannot and does not know most workers in his plant. But even so he must not consider them only as so many people who are on his pay-roll. He can "practice the

---

147 See p. 52, *Supra.*

148 Buber, "Dialogue," *Between Man and Man*, pp. 36–37.

responsibility of dialogue," that is human responsiveness, by thinking of his workers not merely as an extension of his machinery, but "as an association of persons with faces and names and biographies, bound together by a work that is represented by, but does not consist of, the achievements of a complicate mechanism."[149] He must keep alive within himself the potential for human encounter, so that in an actual meeting between himself and one of his employees he will face a man, and not deal with a number.

Buber is aware that management as well as labor may look upon his suggestion as naïve dilettantism. But he feels certain that their protest will turn into approval as soon as they notice what Buber thinks will be the practical results of this new approach to management-labor relations: increased production figures. However, Buber warns ironically, one must not expect that a more human atmosphere in the factory or office will automatically lead to a greater output of goods or work, for "between truth and success there is no pre-stabilized harmony."[150] The life of dialogue cannot be reduced to "procedures" which are experimentally tried out and "pragmatically initiated." The "regulated chaos" in which contemporary society finds itself will not yield to the current mania for "easy mastery of every situation." It will grow into an organic cosmos only through the work of men who perceive the task of the hour, and who respond to it by working towards a breakthrough into the world of Thou which will transform society from a "machina machinarum that turns everything belonging to it into the components of some mechanism" into a "communitas communitatum, the union of the communities into community."[151]

---

149 *Ibid.*, p. 38.

150 *Ibid.*

151 Buber, "Kropotkin," *Paths in Utopia*, p. 39.

# Chapter 4

## ELEMENTS OF DIALOGICAL THINKING IN SOME OTHER PHILOSOPHERS. SIMILARITIES AND DIFFERENCES

Buber is well aware of the fact that the fundamental importance he ascribes to the I-Thou relation is not a new discovery in the history of ideas. He says: "... it has been sensed throughout the ages that man becomes many only by virtue of entering into a relationship, and that the I creates itself in the act of saying Thou."[1]

There is, he feels, "some similarity" between his own thinking and that of Immanuel Hermann Fichte, Friedrich Jacobi, William James, Hermann Cohen, and Ferdinand Ebner. However, he does not make it clear whether this similarity is incidental, or due to an influence of these thinkers upon the development of his own philosophy of dialogue.

While such an influence seems more than likely, there is no conclusive evidence for it in the absence of an explicit statement by Buber himself. Even when he discusses dialogical elements in the work of earlier or contemporary philosophers, he does not acknowledge any indebtedness to them, though he seems to have incorporated some of their relational thought into his own work. The closest he comes to giving credit to someone who might be considered a direct precursor of his philosophy is Ludwig Feuerbach of whom he says: "I myself in my youth was given a decisive impetus by Feuerbach."[2]

Maurice S. Friedman, whose translation and interpretation of much of Buber's work was instrumental in introducing his philosophy to the English speaking world, says that

---

1 Martin Buber, "Nachwort," *Schriften über das dialogische Prinzip* (Heidelberg: Verlag Lambert Schneider, 1954), p. 3, my translation.

2 Buber, "What is Man?" *Between Man and Man*, p. 148.

> Those who arrived at a dialogical or I-Thou philosophy independently of Buber and without influencing him include: Ferdinand Ebner, Gabriel Marcel, Eugene Rosenstock-Huessy, and Franz Rosenzweig. The thought of Marcel, the French Catholic existentialist, bears a remarkable resemblance to Buber's even in its terminology, but, according to Marcel's own statement to Buber when they met in Paris in 1950, he was not influenced by Buber's *Ich und Du* in writing his *Journal Metaphysique*.[3]

Buber himself adds to this list of contemporary or near-contemporary philosophers the names of Hans Ehrenberg, Friedrich Gogarten, Karl Heim, Emil Brunner, Theodor Litts, Karl Löwith, Eberhard Grisebach, and Karl Jaspers. All of them share, he says, the conviction that I and Thou are the primal elements of human existence, and that the dialogical relationship is basic to all "true" living. But he also remarks that there are many areas of disagreement in their work, and that the conclusions at which some of them arrive are often very different from his own.

## 1. Socrates

Tracing relational thinking back to the turn of the eighteenth century only, Buber does not speak of the Socratic dialogues.[4] It would seem, however, that *Socrates* might be considered the dialogical man par excellence. Depending for pursuit of knowledge largely on stimulating contacts with others, he is not a lonely seeker after truth. His search for truth is aided by his search of men's minds: making his fellow-Athenians, whom he engages in thoughtful conversations, the sounding board for some of his own ideas, he also explores with them new ideas as they evolve out of these conversations. The Socratic dialogue with its intellectual give and take serves as a means to attain knowledge, considered to be man's highest virtue.

---

3 M.S. Freidman, "Martin Buber's Theory of Knowledge," *Review of Metaphysics* (December 1954).

4 He refers to Socrates only briefly in a different context, in a discussion of the importance of the I in an I-Thou encounter, as mentioned on p. 32, *Supra*.

Buber's criticism of the It-world of science seems foreshadowed by Socrates' disappointment in the inadequate attempts of physical science to explain "first principles." Socrates, spending his life in "contemplation of true existence" so that he might grasp "the nature of the best" (Phaedo), is not particularly interested in scientific explanations concerning the "how?" of the world. His main interest is to find out the "why?" of the world, and he derives much of his intellectual and psychological support for that quest in the Thou-world of human relationships.

Yet for Socrates there are two roads to knowledge (while for Buber there is only one: encounter). One road traverses dialogical relations, but the other is to be found in solitude. Believing that man may expect to see the truth only with the eye of his soul, Socrates withdraws at certain times from all dialogical contacts and, concentrating upon his own psychic and mental powers, falls into a trance-like state during which he is completely out of touch with the world around him.[5]

Socratic dialectic and Buber's dialogic have certain traits in common. Both presuppose the value of and need for human relatedness, and both play a crucially important role in education as well as in epistemology. But they also differ sharply in essential aspects:

Socratic dialectic is a methodological device for clarifying an issue, or for reaching a clearer understanding of a problem by discussing it. By skillful interrogation, the leader of the dispute assists the participants in expressing their ideas—ideas which supposedly had lain dormant in their souls as innate knowledge. It takes mental alertness (though not necessarily a store of information: see the young boy in "Meno") to stand one's ground when debating with Socrates. Socratic dialectic is an intellectual exercise to train the mind.

In contra-distinction, Buber's dialogic is a state of the human heart and mind.[6]

> The life of dialogue is no privilege of intellectual activity like dialectic. It does not begin in the upper story of mankind. It begins no higher than where humanity begins. There are no

5 Plato, "Symposium," *The Philosophy of Plato,* Jowett translation (New York: The Modern Library, 1956), p. 337.

6 See pp. 37–39, *Supra.*

> gifted and ungifted here, only those who give themselves and those who withhold themselves.[7]

Dialogic is an existential involvement with the Other whom one "means." Dialectic is a somewhat detached matching of wits with the Other whom one means to convince or to persuade. Though Buber admires Socrates for having lived a life "bound up in relation,"[8] he also criticizes "... Socratic irony in which there is inherent a basic remaining unmoved."[9] Dialectic as an intellectual activity is, therefore, merely "thinking towards the other thinker"; but dialogic as a total commitment is "living towards his concrete life."[10]

## 2. Georg Wilhelm Friedrich Hegel

Dialectic is also more than an intellectual activity for *Georg Wilhelm Friedrich Hegel*. It is a law governing all conscious life, a manifestation of "absolute spirit" at work in the historical process through which mankind must go; and it is a method applicable to the development of ideas as well as to the development of individual consciousness in the confrontation of a self and a non-self.

Hegel investigates the gradual growth of man's self-consciousness, that is, his ego or his self, as this self becomes increasingly aware of the existence of the Other, that is another self, another self-consciousness.[11] Hegel's "ego" and "the Other" are not related to each other as I and Thou, yet they, too, depend upon each other for their very existence.

Primitive man, surrounded by nature, may have a vague "self-feeling," a dim instinctual awareness of his physical being. He is, to this extent, indeed conscious. But it takes a long development in the

---

7 Buber, "Dialogue," *Between Man and Man*, p. 35.

8 Buber, *I and Thou*, p. 66.

9 Quoted by S. Maringer, *Martin Bubers Metaphysik der Dialogik im Zusammenhang Neuerer Philosophischer und Theologischer Strömungen: Darstellung und Kritik* (Koln: Buchdruckerei Steiner, Ulrichgasse, 1936) from Buber's "Biblischer Humanismus," an essay in *Der Morgen*, Oct. 1933. My translation.

10 J.L. Blau, "Martin Buber's Religious Philosophy," *Review of Religion*, XIII (1948).

11 G.W.F. Hegel, *The Phenomenology of the Mind*, trans. J.B. Baillie (2nd ed., New York: The Macmillan Co., 1955) Ch. IV, pp. 217ff.

individual's growth to arrive at a state of self-consciousness. Self-consciousness emerges only as man faces man, and the one relates himself to the Other dialectically, as thesis and antithesis. "A self-consciousness has before it a self-consciousness. Only so and only then *is* it self-consciousness in actual fact; for here, first of all, it comes to have the unity of itself in its otherness."[12]

Only by existing for, that is in relation to, an Other does the I become aware of itself. "Ego is the content of the relation, and itself the process of relating."[13] Only by being recognized or acknowledged by an Other self is consciousness transformed into self-consciousness. Thus

> each side is the mediating term to the Other, through which each mediates and unites itself with itself; and each is to itself and to the Other an immediate self-existing reality, which, at the same time, exists thus for itself only through mediation. They recognize themselves as mutually recognizing one another.[14]

But here the similarity between Hegel's and Buber's thought ends. Hegel's self, having found itself through being mediated by the Other, "has lost its own self, since it finds itself as an *other* being"; hence, "it must cancel this, its Other." That is, it must "... sublate the Other independent being in order thereby to become certain of itself as true being." Having cancelled the Other's selfhood (especially in the master-slave relationship, but also in an intellectual collision of two conflicting minds), the ego "proceeds to sublate its own self, for this Other is itself."[15]

The concept of sublation is completely alien to Buber's thought. In a true encounter, even one of antagonists, the opposing individuals do not cancel each other out, nor does one suppress or dominate the Other.[16] He makes him his Thou whose selfhood remains inviolate. And Buber states explicitly that the I, in turn, must not lose its selfhood in the Other being, but preserve its self-identity.[17]

---

12 *Ibid.*, pp. 226–227.

13 *Ibid.*, p. 219.

14 *Ibid.*, p. 231.

15 *Ibid.*, p. 229.

16 See pp. 55 ff, *Supra.*

17 See pp. 42–43, *Supra.*

For Hegel, "consciousness is to itself the truth."[18] For Buber, the I by itself, in isolation, neither is nor has the truth which only an I-Thou encounter yields. For Hegel, the confrontation of self-consciousness with self-consciousness is but a passing stage in the dialectic process, and, like all its fleeting moments, of little lasting account. For Buber, the meeting of I and Thou is an ontologically significant act of being,[19] and the moment is all. It is full of import, the bearer of understanding, knowledge and truth.

When Hegel's two selves meet, one views the Other as potential dialectical opponent; "... an individual makes its appearance in antithesis to an individual."[20] Buber, however, sees men facing each other as potential dialogical partners. Not only is there no implication of an inherent feeling of animosity, but there is an inherent promise of a relationship which will not threaten, but affirm the existence of the I. "A person makes his appearance by entering into relation with other persons."[21]

Hegel is not concerned with the person as person. Man's significance does not lie in his individuality. His historical role is to be a citizen, and his destiny will be shaped not so much by himself as by the state (which is the realization of the divine idea on earth).

For Buber, man as man, as this man, is of central importance. The world radiates out from this man-related-to-an-Other, and the state, as any other institution, derives its meaning and its very *raison d'être* only from the human beings that constitute its membership.

Hegel's dialectic is composed of triads of thesis, antithesis and synthesis, with the thesis and antithesis being absorbed in the synthesis which, in turn, becomes the thesis of a new triad, in an ever ongoing process. But Buber's dialogic, built on the duality of I and Thou, must preserve the juxtaposition of the dual components. For if I and Thou did not remain set over against each other, they could no longer be essentially related. Hegel's dialectic moves forward—while Buber's dialogic moves to and fro.

---

18 Hegel, *The Phenomenology of the Mind*, p. 218.

19 See p. 16, *Supra*.

20 Hegel, *Phenomenology of the Mind*, p. 231.

21 Buber, *I and Thou*, p. 62.

Hegel's dialectical process sweeps the individual along with it towards a set goal. Man is not free to decide whether or not to participate in this process, for he cannot step outside of history. But Buber feels that "the dogma of gradual process is the abdication of man" because it "... leaves no room for freedom."[22] Man's freedom lies in his ability to decide to swim, if necessary, against the fatefully onrushing stream of history, and to become a social and religious reformer who transforms the It of "the dogma of process"[23] into the Thou of personal encounter. He thus changes the face of the world instead of letting himself be shaped by the course of the world.

Buber himself gives no indication that his relational thinking was in any way influenced by, or bears a resemblance to Hegel's analysis of the inter-relatedness of two consciousnesses. He discusses Hegel only as part of a study of the different philosophical approaches to the question "What is Man?"[24] Within this context, he examines Hegel's "logological attempt" to "give man a new security"[25] by placing him in a well-ordered universe where reason reigns supreme. The young Hegel, he says, was still interested in "the unity of the whole man," but "real man will be sought in vain in the later Hegel."[26]

Inasmuch as Buber's foremost concern is with man in his entire being, he rejects a system that isolates and glorifies a partial aspect of man, his rationality. The question "What is Man?" Buber feels, cannot be adequately answered by a philosophy which "can be characterized as the dispossessing of the concrete human person and the concrete community in favour of universal reason, its dialectical processes and its objective structures."[27]

## 3. Ludwig Feuerbach

What Buber's friend and collaborator Franz Rosenzweig was to call their "new thinking" (Das Neue Denken) shortly after the First World

22 *Ibid.*, p. 57.

23 *Ibid.*

24 Included in the volume *Between Man and Man.*

25 Buber, "What is Man?" *Between Man and Man,* p. 139.

26 *Ibid.*, p. 138.

27 *Ibid.*, p. 137.

War seems to have been anticipated by *Ludwig Feuerbach* who wrote in 1843: "True dialectic is not a monologue of the solitary thinker with himself, it is a dialogue between I and Thou."[28] Solitude leads to intellectual sterility, for

> ideas are born only through communication, that is in conversation between man and man. One does not develop concepts, nor even reason as such, by oneself. It takes two individuals to produce a human being—biologically as well as intellectually. Community between man and man is the first principle and criterion of truth and universality.[29]

Feuerbach emphasizes that man's very essence lies in the social structure of the I. An I becomes "real" only by having another I set over against it as a Thou, and by becoming, in turn, a Thou for the other I. Buber apparently agrees that the discovery of the Thou by Feuerbach is "the Copernican revolution" of modern thought, and "an elemental happening which is just as rich in consequences as the idealist discovery of the I."[30]

Through communicating with an Other, a unity is established between I and Thou; but this unity, Feuerbach points out, "rests only on the reality of the difference between I and Thou."[31] The ground from which this unity arises is love, which is much more than an affectionate bond between individuals. It is a means of judging truth, for "where there is no love, there is no truth."[32] Love is also the criterion of the actuality (Wirklichkeit) of existence, for only that which can become an object of love truly exists. "Love is the true ontological proof for the existence (Dasein) of an object external to ourselves (ausser unserem Kopfe)."[33] All being "outside of our head" is relevant only to the degree

---

28 Ludwig Feuerbach, *Grundsätze der Philosophie der Zukunft, Philosophischer Kritiken und Grundsätze,* ed. By Friedrich Jodl, Vol. II (Stuttgart: Friedrich Fromanns Verlag - E. Hauff, 1904), p. 319, my translation.

29 *Ibid.*, p. 304.

30 Buber, "What is Man?" *Between Man and Man*, p. 148, quoted from Karl Heim, "Ontologie und Theologie," *Zeitschrift für Theologie und Kirche,* neue Folge XI, 1930, p. 333; and Karl Heim, *Glaube und Denken*, 1. Auflage (1931), pp. 405ff.

31 Feuerbach, *Grundsätze der Philosophie der Zukunft*, p. 318.

32 *Ibid.*, p. 299.

33 *Ibid.*, p. 298.

in which it affects us; in fact, it exists only to the degree in which it gives us pain or pleasure.

Life's "truth" is disclosed only in the existentially experienced relation between man and the world. This does not mean, though, that Feuerbach places reality within the subject. Reality is, he says, different from that which one only thinks. To prove his point,, he uses Kant's well-known example of the hundred thalers.[34] The hundred imagined thalers "are only in my head." They exist only for me, subjectively. But the hundred real thalers exist for others too, for they can be seen and touched. It is therefore clear that only that exists "objectively" which exists simultaneously for me and for the Other, upon which he and I agree. But though objects exist independently of the subject, they derive their meaning only from the way the subject relates itself to them—a theory which reappears in Buber's philosophy, especially in his treatment of mutuality in the I-Thou relation.[35]

## 4. Henri-Louis Bergson

*Henri-Louis Bergson* is not a dialogical thinker. Yet it seems justified to include his name in this brief survey, because he and Buber share some basic views, starting from similar premises and arriving at similar conclusions. Moreover, Bergson's and Buber's approach to philosophy and to life are very much alike, and there is a strong affinity between their central concepts of intuition and of encounter.

The two philosophers have in common a disbelief in the omnipotence of reason, and both suggest as remedy against the predominance of the rational element in man's life his submersion in the life-stream of the universe. For Buber, this submersion starts with an I-Thou encounter through which man becomes a living part of the cosmic life-force at work in all of creation. For Bergson, this submersion is an act of intuition through which alone man can grasp reality and participate in life's creative evolution. Buber's encounter as well as Bergson's intuition have a quality of ineffability. Encounter as a unique event between an I

34 *Ibid.*, p. 283.

35 See pp. 21 ff, and 48 ff, *Supra*.

and an Other, and intuition as an emphatic transposition of an I into an Other are impervious to a critical investigation of the probing mind.

Both thinkers are agreed that the intellect produces the tools which build society, and that, as such, it is indispensable; but it also has the power to stunt the growth and destroy the living tissue of human relations. Buber's encounter and Bergson's intuition, as the media of and for these human relations, will, it is hoped, rebuild society into a re-created mankind.

Another similarity between the concepts of encounter and intuition lies in their epistemological significance. In Buber's view, man grasps the essence of an Other's being.[36] In Bergson's view, man knows by flowing along with the current of life whose meaning he discerns by intuition. Buber, however, insists on maintaining a distance between I and Thou, while Bergson's intuitive man fuses with the object of his knowledge. For Buber, knowledge is attained by turning towards an Other—man or object—in encounter. For Bergson, knowledge is attained by turning into an Other—through intuition.

## 5. Romano Guardini

The German Catholic priest *Romano Guardini* is a contemporary thinker much occupied with the dialogical principle. He sees in the relation between God and Jesus an eminent exemplification of the I-Thou relation between God and man. Guardini's definition of man, and his subsequent expectation of what man's spiritual attitude and social action should be, closely resemble those of Buber.

"A man is a person called by God. As that man he is capable of answering for his own actions."[37] Man responds to God's call by accepting responsibility for the world. This is an answer only he alone can give, for God addresses each man in his uniqueness as a particular person. Or, rather, man becomes unique as a person only by "facing," that is, by relating himself dialogically to God.

---

36 See pp. 14 ff, *Supra.*

37 Romano Guardini, *The End of the Modern World, A Search for Orientation*, trans. J. Theman and H. Burke (New York: Sheed and Ward, 1956) pp. 81–82.

God is man's point of reference for all existence. "Man is not so constructed as to be complete in himself ... his very essence consists in his relation to God."[38] The immediacy in which man faces a personal God must be carried over into all his other relationships.

Contemporary society suffers from a lack of immediacy: mass media of communication offer a poor substitute for direct relations between man and man. Our machine-dominated age tends to mistake the sensational and the exciting for genuine feeling. We live vicariously—we even kill vicariously. When early man killed another with a club, he experienced his act directly. When modern man pulls a lever in an airplane, releasing a bomb which will destroy thousands of lives, he is still capable of understanding what he is doing, but no longer of "experiencing it as act or event."[39]

Neither are we able any more to experience the acts and events of nature immediately, in awe or in joy. We have lost our ability to address her directly as "Mother Nature." Nature has become "not-natural," an object of scientific research. By the same token, man is becoming "non-human," for humanity is so "purposefully organized" it is losing its human-ness along with its "organic creativity"[40]—a thought very close to Buber's analysis of society in danger of self-destruction because it prefers making a living in the It-world to creating a meaningful life in the Thou-world.

Man as unique person, answerable to God and responsible for his fellow-man, is neither an anonymous member of "the crowd," nor a mere particle swept along inevitably in a "dialectical" or historical process. Guardini feels, as Buber does, that "... no one can estimate in advance the course history will take. One can only step forward to meet it, shape it. History starts anew every minute as long as it is constantly determined anew in the freedom of every individual."[41]

The freedom of the individual consists in his conviction that he can shape history and society by his social action, by "daring to believe that

---

38 Romano Guardini, "Possibilities of Action," *Power and Responsibility: A Course of Action for the New Age*, trans. B. Briefs (Chicago: Henry Regnery Co., 1961), p. 103.

39 Guardini, "The Unfolding of Power," *Ibid.*, footnote p. 41.

40 *Ibid.*, p. 45.

41 Guardini, "The New Concept," *Ibid.*, p. 82.

community is possible, by really opening the doors of the I and not only say 'we,' but to act upon it."[42] For man is dialogical by nature. ("Wir stehen von Natur im Dialog.")[43] The essence of man's existence is "the word" by which he expresses his relation to the Other, and, in the absence of an Other, even to himself; for thinking, too, is speaking.[44]

Man relates himself to man not by pointing indifferently to a "something-there," but through the "dialectic act" of saying Thou. In this act, an I moves away from itself towards an Other. This move from I to Thou is spontaneous, yet man can prepare himself for it by renouncing his naïve ego-centricity. Realizing that he is not the sole hub of the universe, he creates the pre-condition for a genuine Thou-attitude which says: "Over there, too, is a center, and all being exists meaningfully (ist Umwelt) for the other one, too."[45]

This realization must be based on man's ability to set the Other at a distance and to permit him to be and remain himself—a thought which bears a striking resemblance to, but which is spun out, beyond Buber's thought. For Guardini sees society as a complicated system of as many polycentric circles as there are Thous, each overlapping circle representing a private world with its own value judgments, meanings, relationships, and each having a personal claim upon the I. The I responds to these claims by transposing itself out of its own private world of experiencing and understanding into the Other's world. For I and Thou are related "from world to world; from center to center."[46]

---

42 Romano Guardini, "Möglichkeit und Grenzen der Gemeinschaft," *Unterscheidung des Christlichen: Gesammelte Studien* (Mainz: Matthias Grunewald Verlag, 1935), p. 56, my translation.

43 *Ibid.*, p. 59.

44 To illustrate this thesis, Guardini relates this tale: At the court of Emperor Frederic II it was debated whether Hebrew or Latin had been man's original language. In order to find a conclusive answer to this vexing problem, the Emperor arranged for a group of infants to be given the best possible physical care by some carefully selected nurses. However, the women were under strict orders never to say a word to their charges. The experiment failed: the children spoke neither Hebrew, nor Latin. They died.

45 Guardini, "Möglichkeit und Grenzen der Gemeinschaft," *Unterscheidung des Christlichen*, p. 71.

46 *Ibid.*, p. 72.

## 6. Martin Heidegger

That the world-at-large is constituted by intersecting private worlds is an idea similarly expressed by *Martin Heidegger* who asserts that "Dasein is wesenhaft Mitsein."[47] Pointing out the existential-ontological meaning of this phenomenological statement, he explains that all personal existence is existence-with-an-Other, for man's life and his world are always part of an Other's. "Die Welt des Daseins ist Mitwelt. Das In-Sein ist Mitsein mit Anderen. Das innerweltliche Ansichsein dieser ist Mitdasein."[48] Solitude, subsequently, is only a deficient mode of existence.

But Buber finds that Heidegger is not really a relational thinker, because he supposedly sees the individual only in relation to himself, as "human existence in its relation to its *own* being" rather than as "essentially related to something other than himself."[49] Buber also criticizes Heidegger for considering other men as objects of man's solicitude. Solicitude is, to Buber, not a "primal" category of life (as an essential relation is). It is motivated by pity, and though pity inclines one man towards an Other, it forecloses the true mutuality which is needed in an essential relation. Heidegger's man, says Buber, makes his assistance but not his self accessible to the Other. Therefore Heidegger's concept of *Mitsein* is different from Buber's "constitutive principle" of man-with-man. *Mitsein* is, in Buber's rather surprising interpretation, the ultimate of self-being, and therefore a "closed system."

However, Buber, taking an "anthropological view" of man, considers man's being as "an open system"[50] Man's self-being includes all other being, and the essence of man can be understood only if one sees him, as it were, in context.

> Neither the world of things, nor his fellow-man and community, nor the mystery which points beyond these, and also beyond himself can be dismissed from a man's situation. Man can attain

47 Martin Heidegger, *Sein und Zeit* (Tübingen: Max Niemeyer Verlag, 1953), p. 120.

48 *Ibid.*, p. 118.

49 Buber, "What is Man?" *Between Man and Man*, pp. 166–167.

50 *Ibid.*, p. 180.

to existence only if his whole relation to his situation becomes existence, that is, if every kind of living relation becomes essential.[51]

## 7. Some Other Philosophers

Elements of dialogical thinking can be found also in some other philosophical works from the late eighteenth century to the present.

In 1785, *Friedrich Heinrich Jacobi* wrote: "Source of all certainty: you are and I am," and "without Thou there can be no I," meaning by this Thou not only another person, but the external world of objects as well.[52] Buber also mentions *Johann Gottlieb Fichte's* thought, expressed in 1797, that the consciousness of an individual must necessarily be accompanied by that of an Other, of a Thou without which it could not exist.

Being conscious of a Thou creates the wish in the I to enter into a relationship with it. The most elementary as well as the most universal means by which one individual relates himself to an Other is speech. Language becomes the mediator between consciousness and consciousness, as Wilhelm von Humboldt points out in a treatise called "The Dual Number," written in 1827. The need of one being for another is so great that man "longs even for the sake of his mere thinking for a Thou corresponding to the I."[53] Therefore his consciousness separates, as it were, into subject and object during a thought-process in which he is forming a concept. This concept is thought by the subjective part of consciousness which assumes the role of the I, and it is reflected by the objective part which assumes the role of the Thou. It is this drive towards objectivation, this inner urge to juxtapose one's own thought and that of an Other (even though that Other be only one's own objectivated self) which culminates in articulated speech.

51 *Ibid.*, p. 180.

52 Friedrich Heinrich Jacobi, *Briefe über die Lehre des Spinoza,* quoted by J. Cullberg, *Das Du und die Wirklichkeit: Zum Ontologischen Hintergrund der Gemeinschaftskategorie* (Uppsala: Universitets Arsskrift, A.B. Lundequistka Bokhandeln, 1933) Vol. I, p. 25, my translation.

53 Quoted by Buber, "Dialogue," *Between Man and Man*, p. 27.

Thou-consciousness as the basis of all consciousness and of all reality is also characteristic of the work of the Swede *Erik Gustaf Geijer* who wrote, in 1843, that "there is no personality, except in and through another one. Where there is no Thou, there is no I. Therefore the sharpest contrast is not at all constituted by an I and a not-I, but by an I and another I—by an I and a Thou."[54] Geijer attributes Thou-consciousness not only to man, but also to God, "for the Divine Person, too, is unthinkable in isolation ... and if God did not also have a Thou, there would never have been a human being."[55]

It seems safe to assume that *Wilhelm Dilthey*, one of Buber's teachers at the University of Berlin, contributed to the development of Buber's I-Thou theory when he said:

> Understanding is a rediscovery of the 'I' in the 'Thou.' ... This identity of mind in the 'I', in the 'Thou,' in every subject within a community, in every culture ... makes possible the joint result of the various operations performed in the human studies. The knowing subject is here one with its objects.[56]

During the First World War, *Hermann Cohen,* the founder of the Marburg School of Neo-Kantianism, wrote that only the discovery of a Thou makes an I conscious of itself, and that the personality of the I is brought to light by the Thou.

> But is the Thou only another example of the I, and is not a separate discovery of the Thou required even after I have already become aware of my I? Or maybe it is, conversely, that only the Thou, the discovery of the Thou, enables me to become aware of my I, and to arrive at an ethical recognition of my I.[57]

---

54 Quoted by Cullberg, *Das Du und die Wirklichkeit*, p. 28.

55 *Ibid.*, p. 30.

56 Wilhelm Dilthey, *Gesammelte Schriften*, quoted by HM Schulweis, *The Personalistic Philosophy of Martin Buber*, Master's Thesis, New York University, May 1, 1949.

57 Hermann Cohen, *Die Religion der Vernunft aus den Quellen des Judentums*, (Leipzig: Gustav Fock GmbH, 1919), p. 17, my translation.

About the same time, the Austrian philosopher *Ferdinand Ebner* said: "The I and the Thou—these are the spiritual realities of life."[58] I and Thou are bound together by the word, and by love. The word is the objective, love the subjective vehicle of the I-Thou relation. But Ebner's I and Thou are different from Buber's. In Ebner's view, man suffers inescapably from existential loneliness that cannot be relieved by a human Thou. "Only in God, who created man by speaking to him, can man find his Thou: In the deepest recesses of our spiritual life God is the true Thou of the true I in man."[59]

58 Ferdinand Ebner, Das Wort und die geistigen Realitäten. Pneumatologische Fragmente, quoted by J. Cullberg, Das Du und die Wirklichkeit, p. 38.

59 *Ibid.*, p. 38.

# CONCLUSION

In view of the fact that other philosophers have pointed out the significance of the I-Thou relationship, the question arises to what extent Buber's work is original. The originality of a thought is not easily determined. No thinker starts completely without antecedent; he is intellectually nourished by the accumulated ideas of preceding generations. And though he may not consciously borrow from contemporaneous thought he will unconsciously and osmotically absorb it, as he is constantly exposed to its cross-currents.

It is particularly difficult to answer the question of Buber's originality, because he himself fails to make a clear statement about the sources on which he may have drawn for the development of his philosophical concepts.[1] He evidently believes that submission to the spiritual power of an idea which seizes the mind and transforms the thinking of all who encounter its force is more important than recording its origin. As a student will live "in apostleship"[2] of a beloved teacher, perpetuating his influence though he may never even refer to him by name, so a thinker, and especially one as open to the world as Buber is, may pay tribute to the creative mind in general, if not to an author in particular, by building on the intellectual foundations laid by others, or by elaborating an appealing notion found in others.

Moreover, one could argue that in the realm of thought originality is not of decisive importance. The question here should primarily be one of relevance, and not necessarily of newness. It is less important whether a thought has occurred to anyone before than whether its formulation is conducive to man's better understanding of himself; whether its presentation contributes to the clarification and possibly to the solution of human problems; and whether it adds a new perspective to man's outlook upon the world.

All these questions merit an affirmative answer in the case of Martin Buber to whose work (on the assumption that it is not entirely "original") Goethe's dictum is eminently applicable: "The finest sign of

---

[1] See p. 118, *Supra.*

[2] See p. 91, *Supra.*

originality consists in one's ability to develop a received idea in so fruitful a manner that no one else would have discovered how much lay hidden therein."[3]

Buber's impact upon our time is probably best explained not by the originality of the I-Thou concept, but by the originality and fruitfulness with which he treated what he discovered to have lain hidden in it. Also, one might ascribe genuine originality to his development of the I-It concept and its social implications. For by differentiating between the Thou-world and the It-world, Buber has clearly mapped out for man the two realms of his existence which he must bring into proper balance if he is to live meaningfully as an individual and as a member of society.

That is, Buber has created a true "Lebensphilosophie." As such, his work is of deep significance. As a philosophical system, it leaves much to be desired. However, Buber did not set out to create a philosophical system,[4] for he feels that any "system" does violence to the living spirit it tries to capture. For this reason, he made no attempt to arrange his creatively flowing (but sometimes also deplorably meandering) thought methodically.

A philosophical system is, to Buber, just another It which involves only man's intellect and is therefore of little human import. But a *Lebensphilosophie* belongs into or actually creates the Thou-world. It derives its poignancy from the fact that it "says something," in human terms, to man. It is expressive of and provides a guide-line for "lived life."

Buber, who regards thinking not just as an act of cerebration, but as an activity of the "whole man," "an act of his *life*, without any prepared philosophical security,"[5] writes as he suggests man live: spontaneously, unreservedly, personally involved, and out of the immediacy of his own being. And if the profusion of his thought occasionally comes close to

3 Quoted by Leo Baeck, *The Essence of Judaism*, trans. Victor Grubwieser and Leonard Pearl, revised by Irving Howe (New York: Schocken Books, 1948), p. 19.

4 "I have no inclination to systematizing, but I am of course and by necessity a philosophizing man." Quoted by M.S. Friedman, *Martin Buber: The Life of Dialogue*, p. 161, from a letter Buber wrote to him in 1951.

5 Buber, "What is Man?" *Between Man and Man*, p. 124.

resembling confusion, it might be interpreted as merely another approximation of a true life-situation.

Philosophy, according to Buber, should not be considered as a system of several disciplines, such as logic or epistemology, which deal with "partial" questions only. Its concern should be with man in the totality of his "concrete" and "essential" being. This over-all concern with man is characteristic of *"philosophical anthropology"* which, as a method, comes closest to Buber's concept of what philosophy should be. For, unlike a mere "system," philosophical anthropology "is not intent on reducing philosophical problems to human existence and establishing the philosophical disciplines so to speak from below instead of from above. It is solely intent on knowing man himself."[6]

The philosophical anthropologist is more than a detached, objective observer of life. Rather than work out theories, he involves himself in the practical aspects of life, for "only when he does not leave his subjectivity out" can he know "the wholeness of the person"[7]—which is life.

Buber disdains engaging in philosophical speculations about the abstract. Predominantly concerned with and descriptive of "concrete" life situations, his thought may not even be considered to be "pure" philosophy, "if one understands philosophy to be the use of reason as a sufficient means of articulating an ordered, coherent, clear conception of the universe."[8] But if philosophy's "function is to endow the spirit with a creative consciousness of the meaning of human existence,"[9] then Buber's work fully deserves to be called philosophy.

Though it is not a well-structured system, Buber's philosophy presents an internally related body of ideas. But his lack of organization makes for needless and irksome repetitiousness. At times, his literary style is burdened by an ecstatic effusiveness which obscures the clarity of his thought. More often, however, his beautifully poetic formulations

---

6 *Ibid.*, p. 123.

7 *Ibid.*, p. 124.

8 A.A. Cohen, Martin Buber, Studies in Modern European Literature and Thought (New York: Hillary House, 1957), p. 21.

9 Nicholas Berdyaev, *Solitude and Society* (New York: Scribner's Sons, 1938), p. 16.

and the creativity of his language[10] serve as the vehicle of a charismatic personality who bestows significance even on the commonplace.

For Buber does not, as it were, approach words in the It-attitude inherent in conventionally agreed-upon public usage, but in the Thou-attitude of charging them with private meanings. This makes for a style so highly personal that it occasionally seems better suited to the metaphorical world of poetry than to the conceptual world of ideas. There are frequently prophetic overtones—and Buber has, indeed, become almost a prophet to an ever-widening circle of men and women to whose lives his thought has added a new dimension of depth and spiritual richness.

Nor does he detract from his prophetic stature by stating that he felt "impelled by inward necessity" to write "I and Thou" as documentation of a "vision" which he had had since his youth. The vision, at times beclouded, finally "reached steady clarity. This clarity was so manifestly suprapersonal in its nature" that Buber intuitively knew he "had to bear witness to it."[11]

But it is difficult to translate vision into reality, or the experienced Thou into the conceptualized It by which alone its message can be communicated. Almost every philosopher creates his own terminology which must be learned before his work can be understood. But Buber asks more of his reader: he must be able and willing to attune himself to the "speech," the dialogical "word" addressing him through Buber's work, or else the gate to the Thou-world in which Buber lives and out of which he writes will remain locked to him.

However, while the appreciation of a work of art depends to a large degree on the viewer's or listener's ability to project himself into the art-work and to let himself be carried away by its spirit, it is doubtful whether the same principle applies to the understanding of a work of the mind.

Buber appears to share Berdyaev's contention that man's "existence precedes his apprehension of Being, and that this fact determines the quality of his knowledge. He apprehends Being because he himself is

---

10 Buber has rightfully been called a "philosophical poet" by John Cullberg, *Das Du und die Wirklichkeit*, p. 40.

11 Buber, "Postscript to I and Thou," *I and Thou*, p. 123.

part of Being."[12] Consequently, all knowledge and all truth are subjective.

This view, typical of much of existential thinking, has its strong as well as its weak points. Its strength lies in its intellectual honesty and in a certain sense of humility: man does not claim possession of any final answers, exclusive knowledge, or absolute truth. He can, in the last analysis, "really" know only what he "really" experiences—not pragmatically, but existentially. The weakness of this view lies in its easily-made, dangerous assumption that man is the measure of all things. If the truth of the object depends solely on its being experienced by the subject, there are "as many truths as there are subjects,"[13] and one man's experience may well rule out and invalidate an Other's.

The question is whether generally valid theories can be deduced from intensely personal experiences, and whether an existentially experienced truth can be assumed to be a universal truth. If life's truth is to be found only by walking the "narrow ridge" of encounter—dare one make one's own "holy insecurity" into a philosophical principle by which others ought to live? Can dialogic really take the place of epistemology? And is the truth of encounter transmissible to those who did not participate in it?

The subjectivity inherent in existentialism is, to an extent, offset by Buber's religiosity, his belief in an absolute—God, the One, the Eternal Thou.[14] However, he holds that absolutes are beyond man's intellectual grasp. An absolute truth, seen through human eyes, does not change into a relative truth. But the human mind can understand and interpret it only in human terms. And since man's most human terms are I and Thou, he apprehends in and through encounter. "The ultimate truth is one, but it is given to man only as it enters, reflected as in a prism, into the true life-relationships of the human person."[15] Divine truth, experienced through community between man, thus become human

12 N. Berdyaev, *Solitude and Society*, p. 29.

13 Schulweis, *The Personalistic Philosophy of Martin Buber*, p. 36.

14 See p. 75, *Supra.*

15 Buber, "Goethe's Concept of Humanity," *Pointing the Way*, p. 79; see also p. 42, *Supra.*

truth. But "human truth is into conformity between a thing thought and the thing as being; it is participation in Being."[16]

Buber equates truth with the genuineness and authenticity of a dialogically lived life. Truth, therefore, is for him neither objective nor static, but as subjective and dynamic as all of life is; and its sole criterion is "the verifying power of a life-reality."[17] In the existential situation, in his experience of an event or a relation, man's "Erlebnis" becomes his truth, and as *his* truth, it becomes *the* truth.

One of his critics has pointed out, rather irritatedly, that Buber's thought "starts out with subjectivity and ends with subjectivism." He reproaches Buber for equating feeling with knowing, and for confusing what "'he really experiences' with 'he experiences reality.'"[18]

But Buber "starts out with subjectivity" because existence-as-such is subjective—there is no life unless it be lived by a subject. Moreover, Buber's emphasis on the subjective is not motivated by arbitrariness. It should be understood as an emphasis on the spiritual as well as on personal freedom. For only by asserting the individual's "subjective" worth as a person, independent and unique, can man break through the soul-less crowd mentality that threatens to extinguish the spark of the Divine and to obscure the glimpse of the Eternal in his life. As previously discussed,[19] Buber regards objectivity as lack of commitment, and therefore as a human deficiency. But more than that, objectivity is for him a lack of spiritual vitality, and therefore actually an existential deficiency.

To charge Buber with subjectivism would be justified only if he claimed general validity or universal meaning for his private encounters. But he does not—or at least not explicitly. He reiterates again and again that "meanings" are subjective, changing from individual to individual, and that one man's Thou neither need nor can be an Other's. Yet there is a certain ambiguity in Buber's attitude. For while he insists that general theories destroy personal meanings, he does imply—by describing them in detail—that his personal meanings

16 Buber, "Goethe's Concept of Humanity," *Pointing the Way*, pp. 79–80.

17 Buber, "Franz Rosenzweig," *Pointing the Way*, p. 92.

18 Schulweis, *The Personalistic Philosophy of Martin Buber*, pp. 35–36.

19 See pp. 19 and 34, *Supra*.

should be accepted as general theories, or at least as conducive to arriving at general theories. Also, he doubtlessly depends too much on the richly biographical, and too little on the simply logical, in presenting his views.

Sober judgment occasionally balks at the fact that Buber uses descriptions of personal experiences not only as illustrations for a point he wants to make, but in lieu of a point he ought to make. However, his reliance on descriptions is less due to an inability to reason clearly than to his conviction that intellectual concepts cannot adequately convey the feeling-tone of what they "really mean." Their real meaning must therefore be depicted by examples, and one should not, he says, be afraid to delve for these examples into "the innermost chambers" of one's personal life. For want of a better means, Buber uses these examples to

> indicate indirectly certain events in man's life which can scarcely be described, which experience spirit as meeting; and in the end, when indirect indication is not enough, there is nothing for me but to appeal, my reader, to the witness of your own mysteries—buried, perhaps, but still attainable.[20]

Apart from being rather embarrassing in its revivalist overtones, this appeal to the reader only adds to the problematic of the question whether certain events in man's life, by definition ineffable and therefore objectively unverifiable, can serve as instruments of cognition. Buber anticipates at least part of the question by asking whether his personal accounts of I-Thou encounters should be regarded as more than descriptive, "personifying" metaphors. Could he be rightfully accused of a "'mysticism,' blurring the boundaries which are drawn, and which must be drawn, by all rational knowledge"?[21]

Not unexpectedly, he answers that there is no mysticism involved in the "clear and firm structure of the I-Thou relationship" which is quite compatible with reality and with rational thought. I-Thou as "the spirit which lives on in word and work, and the spirit which wishes to

20 Buber, "Postscript to I and Thou," *I and Thou*, p. 127.

21 *Ibid.*, p. 130.

become word and work" can be understood and activated by "everyone with a candid heart and the courage to pledge it."[22]

However, to understand a concept and its practical applicability, and to approve of it as a philosophical principle and as a criterion for truth are not the same. Buber has missed the point of the question. For no matter how well a mood-picture is painted, or how true the description of an existential situation rings to the inner ear, one may still ask whether they are more than a phenomenology of the I-Thou relationship, and whether they will stand the acid-test of intellectual analysis.

Still, Buber's personal impact upon the reader is such that he experiences a sense of identification with the "philosophical poet's" reaction to the world as he encounters it, in spite of occasional serious intellectual misgivings. Criticism on purely rational grounds appears somehow petty or insensitive in view of such statements as: "But the central reality of the everyday hour on earth, with a streak of sun on a maple twig and the glimpse of the Eternal Thou, is greater for us than all enigmatic webs on the brink of being."[23]

Throughout his long life, Buber has preserved a sense of profound wonder at, and an over-fresh delight in, the everyday marvels of existence which he shares with the fascinated reader. This attitude is more than a mere *joie de vivre*. It is an affirmation of all that is—an existential perceptiveness of the grandeur of life with its joy and its sorrow.

Buber's philosophy provides a welcome relief from the near-neurotic concern with feelings of existential anguish, frustration, alienation and guilt which modern man supposedly and inescapably suffers. A generation or an era which tends to look upon all existence as "Sein-zum-Tode"[24] needs to hear a voice which says "you" to life and finds life's deepest meaning in—living. Buber does not deny the fact that all life is, physically, indeed being-towards-death. But he has developed a metaphysics and, subsequently, an ethics which enables man to

22 *Ibid.*

23 Buber, *I and Thou*, p. 87–88.

24 Heidegger, *Sein und Zeit*, Part I, Sec. II, Ch. 1, p. 235ff.

transcend his own biology by making of his life a being-towards-the-Other, that is, a being-towards-life.

Buber's man is no existentially displaced person who, having "lost the feeling of being at home in the world, has lost cosmological security"[25] and is foundering, exposed and alone, in an alien, meaningless world. For Buber provides man with a sense of belonging as he assigns him a place to live: the meeting-ground of I and Thou, a realm of existence whose pivotal point is the Eternal Thou.

In addition to having ontological and therefore philosophical significance, Buber's dialogic serves as corrective for, and bestows a saving grace on, the social conditions of an over-organized and over-mechanized age. He conceives his task to be not the proclamation of a new doctrine, but a "Pointing the Way"[26] towards a richer, more humanly understanding life. He wants to awaken in man an awareness of the Eternal Presence which, as existentially experienced faith, will empower him to live meaningfully in the actual present and cope successfully with its variegated problems.

Sociologists may find his attempt to cure modern man's social ills by the I-Thou remedy somewhat naïve. But if it be naïve, it also is daring and truly "original" to pitch the vulnerable I and Thou of the person against the often invincible-seeming juggernaut of today's many Its. And in the absence of a more sophisticated practical scheme, an all too evidently de-humanized world may find the humanizing possibilities of dialogic well worth exploring.

The scope of Buber's thought is two-dimensional, probing the depth of man's existence, and ranging over the breadth of an amazing variety of subjects. Interested not only in philosophy and religion, but in art, literature, mythology, psychology, education, and sociology as well, Buber has, through his lectures and writings, contributed to a great understanding of the "human factor" in all these fields.

Pledged to a life of "fervor," that is of human involvement, Buber has always held strong convictions. But he also discovered that man's

---

[25] Buber, "What is Man?" *Between Man and Man*, p. 157; see also p. 41–42, *Supra*.

[26] The title given to a collection of Buber's essays, translated and edited by M.S. Friedman, and published in 1957 by Harper Brothers, NY.

> own relation to truth is heightened by the Other's different relation to the same truth—different in accordance with his individuation, and destined to take seed and grow differently. … Men need to see the truth, which the soul gains by its struggle, light up to the Others, the brothers, in a different way, and even to become confirmed.[27]

This generosity of heart and mind cannot fail to strike a chord in the reader. Yet it also presents a problem: what if men do not share Buber's promise that their personal, political, or religious differences of opinion are only different approaches "to the same truth," but if they feel, instead, that they believe in different truths? And if they do believe in different truths—would they not want to convince the Other of his "error"? Is it humanly possible for a man to stand in a genuinely "essential relation" to an Other (as in friendship or love) without wishing to influence him? Moreover, is not all influence an I exerts upon a Thou, even if it be executed by gentle persuasion rather than by imposition, a certain alteration of the Other's otherness—while encounter, by definition,[28] must preserve and confirm the Other's otherness?

This question applies especially to the province of education. Education is, basically, an interference in an Other's life. The educator's stated intent and purpose is to inform the student's mind and mould his character. That is, the educator attempts to change the original state of untutored "otherness" into the best possible approximation of a state of tutored sameness—a sameness of knowledge, behavior, and even outlook defined by the educational goal. If the young person accepts this attempted change of his otherness, all is well. But if he rebels against what he considers unbearable restrictions of his freedom and individuality, the ensuing educational problem will not be solved by "the raising of a finger, perhaps, or a questioning glance"[29] which the gentle philosopher suggests.

Believing in the near-mystical power of encounter, Buber seems to feel that "seeing the other side," or seeing the Other in the totality of his

---

27 Buber, "Distance and Relation," *Psychiatry*, pp. 103–104.

28 See p. 55, *Supra*.

29 Buber, "Education," *Between Man and Man*, p. 89.

being, will prevent any clashes of opinion, or even eliminate any essential differences of opinion between men. But will not, rather, my very insight into the Other's being, my "seeing him as he really is," at times cause me to wish he were different—and that I might contribute to his becoming different?

Coexistence of different personalities or ideologies as Buber envisions it is possible only when people agree to disagree. His belief that even adversaries can have an encounter which will bridge if not dissolve their animosity presupposes an attitude of tolerance and a live-and-let-live spirit on both sides which all too often simply does not exist. A really deeply rooted conviction is usually accompanied by the zealous wish to share it with, if not to impose it upon, the Other—with the express goal of changing the Other's otherness (e.g., religious prophets and missionaries as well as representatives of other "causes"). The ensuing relationship is not one of dialogic, but of a struggle for survival, physically or intellectually.

This is a serious predicament which cannot be written off as belonging into the relationless It-world. Trying to convince the Other of his "wrongness" and to make him accept my "rightness" does not necessarily mean that I wish to reduce him to an It. Quite to the contrary, it may even indicate my fervent desire to make him into a Thou. On the other hand, trying to hold fast to my own "rightness" may be perfectly legitimate, even if it means that I have to fight off the Other's "wrongness." Realistically viewed, some differences between one Weltanschauung and the other go too deep to be dissolved or even bridged by dialogic. Just where man lives most "essentially," he may be least able to establish "essential relations."

But Buber has overcome this predicament (if ever he recognized its existence) in his own life. Deeply convinced that man must never deny an Other a possibility for dialogue, regardless of the Other's lapses not only into silence but even into murderous hostility, Buber has had the personal courage, in at least two historical instances, to defy the public opinion of this own people whose wounds are still too fresh to be healed by any dialogic. First, he has always maintained his conciliatory attitude towards the Arabs,[30] though the majority of Israelis feel that the

30 See pp. 11, *Supra*, "Ichud."

need of the moment can be met only by "Realpolitik" and not by what they regard as a somewhat sentimental idealism.

Secondly, he accepted, after much soul-searching, the Hanseatic Goethe-Prize in Hamburg, in 1951, and the Peace-Prize of the German Book Trade at Frankfurt on Main, in 1953. His moving statements on these occasions showed that his horror of what had happened during the Hitler years was as irradicably burned into his soul, "never-to-be-effaced," as into the soul of his fellow-Jews and all opponents of the Nazi regime. But while they bitterly resented so early a resumption of a dialogue between Germany and a former German Jew, Buber felt that Germany's new generation, together with men of good will everywhere, must search passionately for a "Genuine Dialogue and the Possibilities of Peace."[31]

For without dialogic, runs Buber's message, there will be no peace. And if man fails to create the conditions for a lasting peace, conducive to the spirit of I and Thou, he will have failed as a human being—by having failed his Eternal Thou.

31 Title of Buber's acceptance speech in Frankfurt's Paulskirche, reprinted in *Pointing the Way*, pp. 232 ff.

# BIBLIOGRAPHY

# PRIMARY SOURCES

## Books by Martin Buber

*At the Turning: Three Addresses on Judaism*. (New York: Farrer, Strauss and Young, 1952).

*Between Man and Man*. Translated by Ronald Gregor Smith. (Boston: Boston Press, Beacon Paperback, 1957).

Daniel. Gespräche von der Verwirklichung. (Leipzig: Inselverlag, 1913).

*Eclipse of God: Studies in the Relation between Religion and Philosophy*. (New York: Harper and Brothers, Harper Torchbook, 1957).

*For the Sake of Heaven*. Translated by Ludwig Lewisohn. (Philadelphia: The Jewish Publication Society of America, 1945).

*I and Thou*, Second Edition with Postscript by the Author. Translated by Ronald Gregor Smith. (New York: Charles Scribner's Sons, 1958).

*Ich und Du*. (Leipzig: Inselverlag, 1913).

*The Legend of the Baal-Shem*. Translated by Maurice S. Friedman. (New York: Harper and Brothers, 1955).

*Mamre: Essays in Religion*. Translated by Greta Hort. (Melbourne and London: Melbourne University Press and Oxford University Press, 1946).

*The Origin and Meaning of Ḥasidism*. Translated and edited by Maurice S. Friedman. (New York: Horizon Press, 1960).

*Paths in Utopia*. Translated by R.F.C. Hull. Introduction by Ephraim Fischoff. (Boston: Beacon Press, Beacon Paperback, 1958).

*Pointing the Way*. Translated and edited by Maurice S. Friedman. (New York: Harper and Brothers, 1957).

*The Prophetic Faith*. Translated by Carlyle Witten-Davies. (New York: The Macmillan Co., 1949).

*Reden über die Erziehung*. (Heidelberg: Verlag Lambert Schneider, 1953).

*Die Schriften über das Dialogische Prinzip*. (Heidelberg: Verlag Lambert Schneider, 1954).

*Two Types of Faith*. Translated by Norman P. Goldhawk. (New York: Harper and Brothers, Harper Torchbook, 1961).

## Articles by Martin Buber

"Distance and Relation," translated by Ronald Gregor Smith, *Psychiatry*, Vol. XX, No. 4 (May 1957).

"Elements of the Interhuman," translated by Ronald Gregor Smith, *Psychiatry*, Vol. XX, No. 4 (May 1957).

"Martin Buber on Good and Evil," BBC Television Interview, conducted by Rev. Vernon Sproxton, *Saturday Review*, (April 7, 1962).

## Secondary Sources

## Books

**Agus, Jacob B.** Modern Philosophies of Judaism: A Study of Recent Jewish Philosophies of Religion. (New York: Behrman's Jewish Book House, 1941).

**Berdynev, Nicholas** *Solitude and Society*. Translated by George Reavey. (London: Geoffrey Bles, 1938).

**Bergman, Samuel N.** *Martin Buber: Life as Dialogue*. Translated and edited by Alfred Jospe, in *Faith and Reason: An Introduction to Modern Jewish Thought*. (Washington, DC: B'nai B'rith Hillel Foundations, 1961).

**Berkovits, Eliezer.** *A Jewish Critique of the Philosophy of Martin Buber*. (New York: Yeshiva University, 1962).

**Coates, J.B.** The Crisis of the Human Person: Some Personalist Interpretations. (London: Longmans, Green and Co., 1949).

**Cohen, Arthur A.** Martin Buber: Studies in Modern European Literature and Thought. (New York: Hillary House, 1957).

**Cullberg, Johnb** *Das Du und die Wirklichkeit: Zum Ontologischen Hintergrund der Gemeinschaftskategorie*. Vol. I. (Uppsala: Universitats Arsskrift, 1953; A.B. Lundequistska Bokhandeln, 1933).

**Diamond, Malcolm L.** *Martin Buber: Jewish Existentialist*. (New York: Oxford University Press, 1960).

**Friedman, Maurice S.** *Martin Buber: The Life of Dialogue*. (New York: Harper and Brothers, Harper Torchbook, 1960).

**Herberg, Will.** *Four Existentialist Theologians*. (New York: Doubleday and Co., Doubleday Anchor Book, 1958).

Idem, *Judaism and Modern Man: An Interpretation of Jewish Religion*. (New York: Farrar, Straus and Young, 1951).

Idem, *The Writings of Martin Buber*. (New York: Meridian Books, 1956).

**Kohn, Hans.** *Martin Buber, Sein Werk und Seine Zeit: Ein Versuch über Religion und Politik*. (Köln: Joseph Melzer Verlag, 1961).

**Meringer, Simon.** *Martin Bubers Metaphysik der Dialogik im Zusammenhang Neuerer philosophischer und theologischer Strömungen: Darstellung und Kritik*. (Koln, Buchdruckerei Steiner, Ulrichgasse, 1936).

**Oldhem, Joseph H.** *Real Life is Meeting*. (London: The Sheldon Press; New York: The Macmillan Co., 1947).

**Schulweis, Harold M.** *The Personalistic Philosophy of Martin Buber*. Master's Thesis, New York: New York University, 1948.

## Articles

**Blau, Joseph L.** "Martin Buber's Religious Philosophy, A Review Article," *Review of Religion*, Vol. XIII (1948).

**Freidman, Maurice S.** "Dialogue and the 'Essential We': The Bases of Values in the Philosophy of Martin Buber," *American Journal of Psychoanalysis*, Vol. XX, No. 1 (May 1960).

Idem, "Martin Buber and Christian Thought," *The Review of Religion*, Columbia University Press, Vol. XVIII, No. 1–2 (Nov. 1953).

Idem, "Martin Buber's Philosophy of Education," *Educational Theory*, Vol. VI, No. 2 (April 1956).

Idem, "Martin Buber and the Social Problems of our Time," *Yivo Annual of Jewish Social Science*, Vol. XII (1958–1959).

Idem, "Martin Buber's 'Theology' and Religious Education," *Religious Education*, Vol. LIV, No. 1 (Jan.–Feb. 1959).

Idem, "Martin Buber's Theory of Knowledge," *Review of Metaphysics* (Dec. 1954).

**Kohn, Hans.** "The Religious Philosophy of Martin Buber," *Menorah Journal*, Vol. XXVI, No. 2 (Spring 1938).

**Kurzweil, Zvi E.** "Buber on Education," *Judaism*, Vol. II, No. 1 (Winter 1962).

**Oldham, Joseph H.** "Life as Dialogue," *The Christian News Letters*, Supplement to No. 281 (March 19, 1947).

**Scholem, Gershom.** "Martin Bubers Deutung des Chassidismus," *Neue Zürcher Zeitung*, Literatur und Kunst, Fernausgabe No. 2013 and No. 142 (May 1962).

## Unpublished Material

**Friedman, Maurice S.** *Martin Buber's Life and Thought*. Unpublished Manuscript.

**Levinas, Emmanuel.** *Martin Buber und die Erkenntnistheoric*. Galleyproof of a forthcoming publication.

## Works not by or on Martin Buber

**Bergson, Henri.** *Creative Evolution*. Translated by Arthur Mitchell. (New York: The Modern Library, 1944).

Idem, *Time and Free Will: An Essay on the Immediate Data of Consciousness*. Translated by F.L. Pogson. (London: Muirhead Library of Philosophy, George Allen and Unwin Ltd., 1950).

**Baeck, Leo.** *The Essence of Judaism*. Translated by Victor Grubwieser and Leonard Pearl, revised by Irving Howe (New York: Schocken Books, 1948).

**Cohen, Hermann.** *Die Religion der Vernunft aus den Quellen des Judentums*. (Leipzig: Gustav Fock GmbH, 1919).

**Feuerbach, Ludwig.** *Grundsätze der Philosophie der Zukunft, Philosophische Kritiken und Grundsätze,* Vol. II. Durchgesehen und neu herausgegeben von Friedrich Jodl. (Stuttgart: Fr. Fromanns Verlag [E. Hauff], 1904).

**Guardini, Romano.** *The End of the Modern World: A Search for Orientation.* Translated by J. Theman and H. Burke. Edited with an Introduction by F.D. Wilhelmsen. (New York: Sheed and Ward, 1956).

Idem, *Power and Responsibility. A Course of Action for the New Age*. Translated by E.C. Briefs. (Chicago: Henry Regnery Co., 1961).

Idem, *Unterscheidung das Christlichen. Gesammelte Studien*. (Mainz: Matthias Grunewald Verlag, 1935).

**Hagel, Georg Wilhelm Friedrich.** *The Phenomenology of the Mind*. Translated by J.B. Baillie. (New York: The Macmillan Co., 1955).

**Heidegger, Martin.** *Sein und Zeit*. (Tübingen: Max Niemeyer Verlag, 1953).

**Plato.** *The Works of Plato*. The Jowett Translation. Edited and with an Introduction by Irwin Edman. (New York: The Modern Library, 1956).

www.ingramcontent.com/pod-product-compliance
Lightning Source LLC
Chambersburg PA
CBHW060619310726
48982CB00003B/604

*9781618112651*